Diabetic Dream Desserts

Also by Sandra Woodruff

Secrets of Good-Carb/Low-Carb Living

The Complete Diabetes Prevention Plan

The Good Carb Cookbook

The Best-Kept Secrets of Healthy Cooking

Secrets of Fat-Free Baking

Secrets of Fat-Free Cooking

Diabetic Dream Desserts

More Than 130 Simple and Delicious

Reduced-Sugar Dessert Recipes

Sandra Woodruff

Avery

a member of Penguin Group (USA) Inc.

New York

a member of
Penguin Group (USA) Inc.
375 Hudson Street
New York, NY 10014
www.penguin.com

Library of Congress Cataloging-in-Publication Data

Woodruff, Sandra L.
Diabetic dream desserts : more than 130 simple and delicious
reduced-sugar dessert recipes / Sandra Woodruff.
p.   cm.
Rev. ed. of 1997 publication.
ISBN 1-58333-201-4
1. Diabetes—Diet therapy—Recipes.   2. Desserts.   I. Title.
RC662.W66   2004   2004047467
641.8'6—dc22

Printed in the United States of America
1   3   5   7   9   10   8   6   4   2

Book design by Meighan Cavanaugh

Illustrations by John Wincek

Dedicated to my favorite taste testers,

Wiley, C.D., and Belle

Acknowledgments

It has been a pleasure to produce this book with the professionals at Avery publishing, who have lent their support and creativity at every stage of production. Special thanks go to John Duff for providing the opportunity to produce this new edition of *Diabetic Dream Desserts* and to my editor, Dara Stewart, whose ongoing support and attention to content, clarity, and consistency are greatly appreciated.

A big thanks also goes to the friends and family members who have lent their enduring support and encouragement, and to my clients and colleagues, whose ideas and questions inspire me to continue learning and experimenting with new things.

Contents

Introduction

Making and eating great food is one of life's simplest and greatest pleasures. And homemade desserts frequently top the list of favorites. Cookies fresh from the oven, bubbling cobblers and fruit crisps, warm and yeasty coffee cakes and buns, and sweet and delicious cakes and pies have warmed the hearts of generations. Homemade treats are also a special part of many family traditions as treasured recipes are passed from parent to child with loving care. Just the aroma of freshly baked cookies, breads, cakes, and other treats can bring back the memory of special times.

Unfortunately, dessert poses a real dilemma for people with diabetes. Besides having an urgent need to control carbohydrates and calories, people with diabetes must also choose their dietary fats with care. Is it even possible to enjoy dessert under these circumstances? Absolutely. *Diabetic Dream Desserts* will show you how.

This newly revised edition of *Diabetic Dream Desserts* retains some of my all-time favorite recipes from the previous work, with an update to reflect the latest developments in diabetes management, the availability of new products that have entered the marketplace, and cooking techniques that simplify and streamline food preparation. In addition, this new edition features more than seventy totally new, never-before-published recipes that will be sure to delight family and friends alike.

The past several years have greatly reinforced and enhanced our understanding of the role of diet in treating—and even preventing—diabetes. New discoveries about carbohydrates, fats, fiber, and many other nutrients make it possible to maximize the benefits of nutrition therapy more than ever. *Diabetic Dream Desserts* incorporates the newest principles in diabetes management and helps you put them into practice in your everyday life. For instance, recipes feature more "good carbs" like fruits, oats, and whole-grain flours whenever possible, while cutting back on ingredients like white flour and sugar. Emphasis also placed on using healthful fats like vegetable oils, trans-free margarines, nuts, and seeds, while limiting harmful saturated and trans fats. Just as important, every effort has been made to keep calories under control by using lower-fat ingredients and creative cooking techniques whenever possible.

Diabetic Dream Desserts begins by explaining how sugar, fat, fiber, and other nutrients affect diabetes, and how smart eating can promote optimal health. You'll then learn how to use whole-grain flours, fruits, fruit juices, spices, various sweeteners, the best fats and oils, and even some convenience items to create wholesome and delicious treats that will help you maximize nutrition. The remainder of the book presents a fabulous selection of delectable cakes, pies, puddings, cookies, cobblers, crisps, dessert breads, and other sweet treats that are sure to please. It is my hope that *Diabetic Dream Desserts* will prove that treats do not have to be full of sugar, fat, and calories—and that lighter, more wholesome goodies can be delicious, satisfying, and immensely enjoyable for the entire family.

1. Having Your Cake and Eating It, Too

Sometimes you can have your cake and eat it, too . . . and your pies, cobblers, crisps, puddings, and cookies. This book presents recipes for a variety of delectable desserts prepared in accordance with the latest diabetes guidelines. Emphasis is placed on using low to moderate amounts of sugar and healthful fats, and keeping calories under control. Many of the recipes also incorporate healthful whole grains, fruits, and other nutritious fiber-rich foods.

This chapter begins by explaining what diabetes is and how sugar, fat, fiber, and other nutrients affect this largely preventable and treatable disease. Following this, you will learn about the various ingredients that are featured in the recipes throughout this book. You will also learn about some tips and techniques that will allow you to modify your own favorite recipes and create a dazzling array of satisfying and delicious treats.

Diabetes and Your Diet

In simple terms, diabetes is a disorder that causes blood sugar levels to become abnormally high. This disease centers on the hormone insulin and the way in which the body metabolizes food.

Eating sets off a complex series of events. As food moves from the mouth to the stomach to the intestines, it is systematically broken down, and its carbohydrates, proteins, and fats are released. As sugar enters the bloodstream in the form of glucose, blood sugar levels rise. At this point, the pancreas normally secretes insulin, which transports sugar from the blood into the cells. There it can be used for energy or stored for later use. But when someone has diabetes, either the pancreas does not make enough insulin to handle dietary sugar or the cells do not respond to the insulin. As a result, the sugar stays in the blood instead of entering the cells, and the cells become starved for energy. People who do not control their diabetes have chronically elevated blood sugar levels. Over a number of years, this can lead to serious complications such as cardiovascular disease, nerve damage, kidney disease, blindness, and amputations.

While diabetes can be a devastating disease, it is also one of the most preventable and treatable. The vast majority of people who develop diabetes have the kind known as *type 2* diabetes. In the past, type 2 diabetes was called *adult-onset* diabetes because it typically struck people over age forty. This is no longer the case though, as more and more young adults and even children are developing this disease. In fact, type 2 diabetes is quickly becoming one of the biggest epidemics of our time. What's behind this alarming trend? Type 2 diabetes is strongly linked to being overweight, having poor dietary habits, and a sedentary lifestyle. Positive changes in nutrition and physical activity are often all that are needed to keep diabetes in check. Through sensible eating and regular exercise, many people who are at high risk for developing diabetes can also stop it before it starts. The following pages describe how various foods and nutrients affect diabetes, and how you can make your diet work for you.

Sugar and the Diabetic Diet

The most obvious change that people think of when planning a diabetic diet is to eliminate sugar. And while no one can argue that sugar is health food, research has demonstrated that completely doing away with sugar is not necessary. In fact, most people with diabetes can include *some* sugar in their diets.

How much sugar is acceptable? For the general population, it is recommended that no more than 10 percent of calories come from refined, simple sugars like white table sugar. This means that a person who needs 2,000 calories per day to maintain his or her weight should consume no more than 50 grams per day (about 12½ teaspoons) although less would be better. About half this amount—6 teaspoons per day—would be prudent for people with diabetes. Be sure to check with your health-care provider to learn exactly how much sugar is acceptable in your diet.

When including sugar or sugary sweets in a diabetic diet, it's vital to *substitute* the sugar for other carbohydrates, rather than simply adding it to your meal plan. Why? The amounts and types of foods prescribed by your dietitian are related to your weight-management goals and to any medications you are taking such as insulin or diabetes pills. Foods eaten in excess of those prescribed in your meal plan can raise your blood sugar levels and cause weight gain.

Also keep in mind that despite the fact that some sugar is allowable in a diabetic diet, it's still prudent to keep your sugar intake to a minimum. After all, sugar is a nutrient-poor food. And eaten in excess, sugar can actually deplete your body of the B vitamins, chromium, and other important nutrients it needs to metabolize carbohydrates. Too much sugar can also raise levels of blood triglycerides and lower HDL (good) cholesterol, which is already a problem for many people with diabetes. And of course, most sweets contain more than just sugar—saturated fat and refined flours are usually other prominent ingredients. These foods should be limited in any healthy diet.

Most of the recipes in this book contain 25 to 75 percent less refined sugar than traditional, nondiabetic recipes. Ingredients like fruit, fruit purees, and dried fruits add natural sweetness to recipes. Flavorings and spices like vanilla, nutmeg, cinnamon, and orange rind are used to enhance sweetness, reducing the need for added sugar. And mildly sweet grains like oats, oat flour, and whole-wheat pastry flour also reduce the need for sugar while adding their own unique nutritional benefits.

Carbohydrates and the Glycemic Index

The glycemic index (GI) is a system that was developed in the 1980s to rank carbohydrate-containing foods based on how quickly they turn into sugar after they are eaten. In a nutshell, the higher the GI of a food, the faster the resultant rise in blood sugar after eating it. Low-GI foods, on the other hand, are slowly digested and absorbed, allowing for a gradual rise in blood sugar levels.

Foods that tend to rank high on the glycemic index include sugary sodas and many sweets; white bread; processed breakfast cereals; processed snack foods like chips, crackers, and pretzels; and baked, french-fried, and mashed potatoes. In contrast, vegetables, fruits, legumes, whole grains, and dairy products tend to rank low on the glycemic index.

In recent years, the glycemic index has received a lot of attention with regard to treating diabetes, obesity, heart disease, and various other conditions. A number of studies have found that eating low on the glycemic index can help people maintain better blood sugar control, lower blood triglycerides, and raise HDL (good) cholesterol. In addition, low-GI foods may foster better weight control by helping to stave off between-meals hunger. In light of this evidence, diabetes guidelines in Australia, Canada, and Europe recommend that people substitute more "slow-release" low-GI carbohydrates for the high-GI foods in their diet. Of course, the *amount* of carbohydrate eaten also has to be considered—since eating super-sized portions of low-GI foods will most certainly lead to increased blood sugar levels and weight gain.

What does all this have to do with diabetic desserts? You can lighten your glycemic load and improve your health outlook by choosing treats that emphasize more low-GI "good" carbs. For instance, low-sugar fruit pies in an oatmeal crust, fruit crisps with oat and nut toppings, and low-sugar puddings and custards are much better choices than cakes and cookies made with lots of white flour and sugar. This is not to say that you can't *ever* eat high-GI foods, but they should be put into proper perspective. Later in this chapter, you will learn about some ingredients that can help you create a wide variety of treats that are lower in sugar, higher in nutrition, and delicious enough to serve to friends and family alike.

THE ROLE OF FAT

Too much fat—especially artery-clogging *saturated* fat—is a big problem in many people's diets. This is especially worrisome for people with diabetes who have a much higher risk for heart disease than nondiabetics. Adding fuel to the fire, fat is a very concentrated source of calories (9 calories per gram) compared to carbohydrate or protein (4 calories per gram). This is why high-fat foods like milk, cheese, meat, mayonnaise, and salad dressing frequently have twice the calories of their low- and no-fat counterparts.

How much fat is appropriate for a diabetic diet? A healthy range for fat intake can be anywhere from 20 to 35 percent of calories, depending on your personal health and weight-management goals. Your dietitian can provide a personalized nutrition prescription. The recipes in this book will help you keep your fat intake within healthy limits. The following inset explains the basics of what you should know about dietary fat and the latter part of this chapter will help you choose the best fats for long-term health.

Dietary Fats 101

Few topics in nutrition can boggle the mind like that of dietary fats. Knowing the difference between saturated, trans, monos and polys, omega-3s and omega-6s can indeed be confusing! But if you have diabetes, it's especially important to know the "good" fats from the "bad." To put things in perspective, here are the basics you should know about fats.

SATURATED FAT
Saturated fats are associated with insulin resistance and a higher diabetes risk. Saturated fats also elevate LDL (bad) blood cholesterol levels and raise the risk for cardiovascular disease. Fatty meats; high-fat dairy products like whole milk, butter, cream, full-fat cheese, ice cream, and full-fat sour cream; and coconuts are all high in saturated fat. Saturated fat is often easy to spot because it is solid at room temperature (like the fat around a steak, in a strip of bacon, or a stick of butter).

TRANS FAT

This fat is formed when liquid vegetable oils are hydrogenated to make them more solid. Trans fats behave like saturated fats in the body and may in fact be even worse for your health. Trans fats are linked to insulin resistance and diabetes. One study found that a diet high in trans fat increased diabetes risk by 31 percent. Like saturated fats, trans fats also raise LDL (bad) cholesterol. In addition, they lower HDL (good) cholesterol, posing a dual risk for cardiovascular disease.

Trans fats are found in partially hydrogenated vegetable oils, vegetable shortenings, and hard margarines. Commercial bakery items, processed snack foods, fried foods, and other foods that contain shortening or hydrogenated vegetable oils are also big offenders.

MONOUNSATURATED FAT

Popularized by the heart-healthy "Mediterranean diet," monounsaturated fats have become a staple in many people's diets. Olive oil is the best-known source of monounsaturated fat, but canola oil, avocadoes, and most nuts are rich in monounsaturated fats as well. While monounsaturates are a healthful choice, remember that they are still a concentrated source of calories, so include them in your diet with your weight-management goals in mind.

POLYUNSATURATED FAT

Two types of polyunsaturated fats, known as *omega-6* and *omega-3,* are essential for life. The ratio of these two fatty acids in your diet is also important because they have very powerful and very opposing effects in the body. Researchers believe that humans evolved on a diet that provided about equal amounts of omega-6 and omega-3 fats. Modern diets, however, which are based on grain-fed meats and hydrogenated oils, supply up to 20 times as much omega-6 as omega-3 fat. This imbalance favors the development of cardiovascular disease and may also promote cancer, inflammatory diseases like rheumatoid arthritis, and autoimmune disorders like lupus.

How can you get more omega-3 fats? Fatty fish is the best source of some especially potent omega-3 fats known as EPA and DHA. Among plant foods, flaxseeds and flax oil are the most concentrated sources. Canola oil, walnuts, and soy are also good sources of this essential fat.

THE ROLE OF FIBER

Study after study supports the benefit of high-fiber foods in preventing obesity, diabetes, heart disease, and cancer. Yet most of the fiber—along with essential nutrients, antioxidants and phytochemicals—is processed out of carbohydrate-rich foods today.

Viscous or *soluble* fibers found in foods like oats, legumes, barley, and many vegetables and fruits, may be especially beneficial for people with diabetes. These foods are slowly digested and absorbed, resulting in lower blood glucose and insulin levels. They also create a sensation of fullness that helps prevent overeating.

The fiber in whole-grain breads and cereals also appears to protect against diabetes. One reason may be that these foods are rich in magnesium, which is associated with improved insulin sensitivity. Another reason may be that people who eat plenty of whole grains and other high-fiber foods tend to be thinner than people who eat diets high in refined carbohydrates.

How much fiber should you eat? Health experts recommend eating at least 25 to 35 grams daily (most people get only half this amount). Diets that provide up to 50

Fiber and Selected Nutrients in Various Flours and Grains

FLOUR OR GRAIN (1 CUP)	DIETARY FIBER (GRAMS)	CALCIUM (MG)	MAGNESIUM (MG)	POTASSIUM (MG)	ZINC (MG)
White flour	3	19	27	134	<1
Whole-wheat flour	16	41	166	486	3.5
Oat flour	12	47	134	317	2.8
Rolled oats	10	42	120	283	2.5
Oat bran	14	54	221	532	2.9
Wheat bran	25	42	354	686	4
Wheat germ	15	51	362	1,070	19

grams of fiber daily have been found to be even more beneficial for blood glucose, insulin, and cholesterol levels.

Made properly, fruit desserts, pies, quick breads, cookies, and cakes can provide a respectable amount of fiber. One way to increase fiber is to replace part or all of the white flour with a whole-grain product. To show what a big difference this little change can make, the table on page 9 compares the fiber and nutrient content of various flours and grains.

VITAMINS, MINERALS, AND OTHER ESSENTIAL NUTRIENTS

A plethora of vitamins, minerals, antioxidants, and phytochemicals are critical for optimal health. Some of these nutrients—such as chromium, magnesium, zinc, and B vitamins—play essential roles in the body's handling of blood sugar. Others, including a variety of antioxidants and phytochemicals, help prevent diabetic complications like heart and vascular disease.

Because many people eat highly refined and overly processed diets, they do not get nearly enough essential nutrients. A healthful, well-balanced diet is the first line of defense against nutritional deficiencies. This means eating generous amounts of vegetables and fruits; choosing whole grains instead of refined versions; choosing lean meats and low-fat dairy products; and emphasizing healthful oils, nuts, and seeds as your main sources of dietary fat. With just a little forethought, a variety of treats and desserts can also be enjoyed as part of your healthy eating plan.

As you have seen, sugar is not the only factor that is important when planning a diabetic diet. Fat, fiber, and a myriad of nutrients must also be considered when planning your healthy diet. In the remainder of this section, you will become acquainted with some ingredients that will help you trim excess sugar and fat from your diet and maximize the fiber and nutrients.

About the Ingredients

The recipes in this book will allow you to make goodies that not only are delicious, but also will work well in your meal plan. In the pages that follow, we'll take a look at the ingredients that can help make virtually any dessert a dream.

Low-fat and Nonfat Dairy Products

A wide range of nonfat and low-fat dairy products are available, making it possible to create deceptively rich cheesecakes, parfaits, puddings, and dessert fillings. Here are some of the dairy products used throughout this book.

Buttermilk

Buttermilk adds a rich flavor and texture to muffins, cakes, quick breads, and many other recipes. Originally a by-product of butter making, this product should perhaps be called "butterless" milk. Most brands of buttermilk contain from 0.5 to 2 percent fat by weight, but some contain as much as 3.5 percent fat. Choose brands that contain 1 percent or less fat.

If you do not have buttermilk on hand, you can make a good substitute by mixing equal parts of plain yogurt and nonfat milk. Alternatively, place a tablespoon of white vinegar or lemon juice in a one-cup measure and fill to the one-cup mark with nonfat milk. Let the mixture sit for 5 minutes before using. Most grocery stores also sell buttermilk powder alongside the nonfat dry milk. Use it according to manufacturer's directions.

Cream Cheese

Regular full-fat cream cheese contains 10 grams of fat per ounce, making an eight-ounce block the equivalent of a full stick of butter! A better alternative is reduced-fat cream cheese (Neufchâtel), which contains 40 percent less fat. The reduced-fat cheese can be used in cheesecakes, frostings, fillings, and other recipes just as you would regular cream cheese. Nonfat cream cheese, which contains no fat at all, can also star in many dessert recipes, but because it has a higher water content, you may need to modify the recipe somewhat to get good results. The recipes in this book are developed specifically for use with the lower-fat products and will specify which type of cream cheese should be used for best results.

Evaporated Milk

Evaporated milk is available in both fat-free and lower-fat versions. This ingredient can replace cream in custards, puddings, and other dishes, where it adds creamy richness, calcium, protein, and other nutrients, but not a lot of fat. If you don't have any evaporated fat-free milk on hand, you can make a substitute by placing ⅓ cup of nonfat dry milk powder in a one-cup measure and filling it to the one-cup mark with nonfat or low-fat milk.

Milk

Whole milk, the highest-fat milk available, is about 3½ percent fat by weight and has 8 grams of fat per cup. This may not seem all that bad until you consider that a gallon of milk contains about 1½ sticks of butter! Instead, choose nonfat (skim) milk, which contains less than a half gram of fat per cup. Your next best choice is 1 percent (low-fat) milk, with about 2 grams of fat per cup.

Nonfat Dry Milk Powder

Like evaporated nonfat or low-fat milk, nonfat dry milk powder can add extra richness to custards and puddings while boosting nutritional value. This ingredient can also be added to low-sugar cookies, quick breads, and other baked goods to enhance browning and flavor.

Ricotta Cheese

Ricotta is a mild, slightly sweet, creamy cheese that may be used in cheesecakes, frostings, puddings, and dessert fillings. As the name implies, nonfat ricotta contains no fat at all. Light and part-skim brands are available with about 4 to 6 grams of fat per quarter cup. An equal portion of whole-milk ricotta, on the other hand, contains about 8 grams of fat.

Soft-Curd Farmer Cheese

This soft, slightly crumbly white cheese makes a good low-fat substitute for cream cheese in many recipes. Most brands have about 3 grams of fat per ounce compared with 10 grams for cream cheese. Some brands are made from whole milk, so read labels before you buy.

Sour Cream

As calorie- and fat-conscious folks know, full-fat sour cream contains almost 500 calories and 48 grams of fat per cup! Use the nonfat version though, and you'll trim all of the fat and about half the calories. Made from nonfat milk thickened with vegetable gums, this product can substitute nicely in a wide variety of dazzling desserts. If you don't care for nonfat brands, choose a reduced-fat or light brand, which will have 25 to 50 percent less fat.

Yogurt

Many flavors of yogurt are available that are low in both sugar and fat, making this a versatile ingredient for your diabetic dream desserts. Light yogurt can star in mousses, puddings, parfaits, creamy pie fillings, and many other recipes where it adds creamy richness as well as calcium, protein, and other important nutrients. You can also mix a quarter to a third part light vanilla (or other flavors) of yogurt into nonfat or light whipped topping to enhance texture and flavor.

Yogurt Cheese

A good substitute for cream cheese in cheesecakes, frostings, and fillings, yogurt cheese can be made at home with most brands of plain or flavored yogurt that do not contain gelatin or thickeners such as carrageenan or guar gum. Simply place the yogurt in a funnel or a coffee filter lined with cheesecloth and let it drain into a jar in the refrigerator overnight. When the yogurt is reduced by half, it is ready to use.

FATS AND OILS

Most people are surprised to learn that fats like vegetable oils, margarine, and butter often contribute more calories to desserts than sugar does. And sugar-free and low-carb recipes frequently top the list of high-fat desserts. The reason? It's a real challenge to trim both sugar and fat from dessert recipes and still maintain an appealing flavor and consistency. For this reason, extra fat is often added to low-sugar recipes to compensate for the texture and taste that is lost when sugar is removed.

That said, smart cooks who know a few tricks of the trade *can* create low-sugar treats that are also quite moderate in fat. And when you do use fat, some choices are far better than others. The following section presents some of the best for your diabetic dessert recipes.

Canola Oil

Low in saturated fats and rich in monounsaturated fats, canola oil contains alpha-linolenic acid, an essential omega-3 fat that is deficient in most people's diets. For these reasons, canola oil should be one of your primary cooking oils. Canola oil has a very mild, bland taste, so it is a good all-purpose oil for cooking and baking when you want no interfering flavors.

Soybean Oil

Most cooking oils that are simply labeled *vegetable oil* are made from soybean oil. This oil supplies a fair amount of omega-3 fat, though not as much as canola and walnut oils do. Like canola oil, soybean oil has a bland flavor that works well in dishes where you want no interfering flavors.

Walnut Oil

With a delicate nutty flavor, walnut oil is an excellent choice for baking, cooking, and salads. Like canola oil, walnut oil contains a substantial amount of omega-3 fat. Most brands of walnut oil have been only minimally processed and can turn rancid quickly, so once opened, they should be refrigerated.

Olive Oil

Although it's strong flavor is not appropriate for most dessert recipes, olive oil is an excellent choice for your other cooking needs. Rich in monounsaturated fat, olive oil also contains phytochemicals that help lower blood cholesterol levels and protect against heart disease and cancer. Unlike most vegetable oils, which are very bland, olive oil adds its own delicious flavor to foods. Extra virgin olive oil is the least processed and most flavorful type of olive oil. It also has the highest nutritional value. What about "light" olive oil? In this case, the oil is more processed to develop a lighter flavor, which is mild and bland compared with that of extra virgin oils.

Nonstick Vegetable-Oil Cooking Spray

Available in both plain and butter flavors, these products are pure fat. The advantage to using them is that the amount that comes out during a one-second spray is so small that it adds an insignificant amount of fat to a recipe. Nonstick cooking sprays are very useful to the low-fat cook to promote the browning of foods and to prevent foods from sticking to pots and pans. Choose brands made with canola, soybean, or olive oil.

A Smart Way to Slash Fat

Looking for a way to slash the fat in baked goods? Try replacing the butter, margarine, or other solid shortening with half as much oil. For instance, if a recipe calls for ½ cup of butter, substitute ¼ cup of oil. Bake as usual, checking the product for doneness a few minutes before the end of the usual baking time. This technique makes it possible to produce moist and tender cakes, breads, and biscuits, crisp cookies and tender piecrusts—all with about half the original amount of fat. For the most nutrition, be sure to use one of the oils recommended in this chapter.

MARGARINE

In the past, many margarines contained unacceptable amounts of hydrogenated vegetable oils and harmful trans fats. All that is changing as more and more trans-free brands are becoming available. Look for soft, trans-free margarines made with canola, soybean, and/or olive oil. When the recipes in this book call for margarine, it means a regular (full-fat) version with 9 to 11 grams of fat per tablespoon. When a recipe calls for reduced-fat margarine, choose a brand that contains 5 to 6 grams of fat per tablespoon.

Using Reduced-Fat Margarine and Light Butter in Baking

Contrary to popular belief, reduced-fat margarine and light butter can be used in some recipes. However since the reduced-fat products contain more water, they usually cannot be substituted on a one-for-one basis with the full-fat product. The general rule is to replace full-fat margarine or butter with two-thirds to three-quarters as much of the reduced-fat product. For instance, if a recipes calls for ½ cup of margarine or butter, try using just 5 or 6 tablespoons of a reduced-fat brand.

Some of the recipes in this book give you an option of using either reduced-fat margarine or the full-fat version. This will allow you to create treats that best suit your taste and nutritional preferences. Other recipes are specifically designed to use a small to moderate amount of regular margarine, and cutting fat any further could compromise the quality of the finished product. The inset above provides guidelines on how to substitute reduced-fat margarine or light butter in your own recipes.

Butter

The bad press that margarine has received in recent years has caused many people to switch back to butter. And while butter may be a slightly better choice than a hard, trans-packed margarine, it is still loaded with artery-clogging saturated fat. The bottom line is that neither high-trans margarines nor butter should play a prominent role in a healthy diet. The recipes in this book give you a choice of using margarine or butter. A soft, trans-free margarine as described above, should be your first choice. Butter should be saved for a once-in-a-while treat.

Eggs

Everyone who bakes knows that eggs are indispensable in a wide range of dessert recipes. Most people also know that eggs are loaded with cholesterol—just one large egg uses up two-thirds of your daily cholesterol budget. One egg also contains 5 grams of fat. The good news is, it's a simple matter to make dishes with more whites (which are fat- and cholesterol-free) and fewer yolks to create cholesterol-free or reduced-cholesterol versions of your favorite foods.

Although whole eggs are high in cholesterol, most health experts agree that a healthy diet can include four to seven egg yolks per week. Having said that, people with diabetes appear to be more sensitive to dietary cholesterol, so ask your physician or dietitian to make a recommendation for your specific needs. When you do use whole eggs, look for omega-3 enriched brands. These eggs come from hens that eat a diet enriched with ingredients like flaxseed, marine algae, and fishmeal. As a result, the eggs contain more beneficial omega-3 fats. Some are also higher in vitamin E and other nutrients.

EGG SUBSTITUTES

Contrary to what the term "substitute" implies, egg substitutes are made from 99 percent pure egg whites. The remaining 1 percent consists mostly of vegetable thickeners and yellow coloring—usually beta-carotene or the plant-based coloring agents annatto or turmeric. Egg substitutes are convenient to use and can help you create lower-fat, cholesterol-free versions of many of your favorite foods. You will find egg substitutes in both the refrigerated foods section and the freezer case of your grocery store.

GRAINS AND FLOURS

Just because a food is low in sugar or fat does not mean it is necessarily good for you. Foods high in white flour and other refined grains provide few nutrients and can be harmful to your health when eaten in excess. Whole grains and whole-grain flours, on the other hand, contain a multitude of nutrients such as vitamin E, zinc, magnesium, and chromium that are essential for excellent health.

Once accustomed to the heartier taste and texture of whole grains, most people prefer them to tasteless refined grains. Here are some whole-grain products that you may find useful as you create healthier treats. To prevent rancidity, store these ingredients in the refrigerator or freezer.

Flax

Loaded with healthful omega-3 fats, flaxseeds can be ground in a blender or coffee grinder into flax meal, which can replace up to 25 percent of the flour in muffins, quick breads, and other recipes. (Note: Flax experts recommend limiting intake to 1 tablespoon of ground flaxseed per day until more is known about the health effects of consuming larger amounts.) Once ground, flax should be kept refrigerated and used within a few weeks.

Oatmeal

Oats are loaded with cholesterol-lowering soluble fiber, high in nutrition, and provide slow-release (low-glycemic index) carbohydrate that helps keep blood sugar levels more stable. You can replace part of the flour in muffins, quick breads, and other recipes with oatmeal for a fiber and nutrition boost. For the most health benefits, avoid *instant* oats, which are very thinly cut and more processed. Both old-fashioned (five-minute) and quick-cooking (one-minute) oats are used in the recipes in this book. Each recipe will specify which kind of oats to use.

Oat Bran

The outer part of the oat kernel, oat bran is a concentrated source of cholesterol-lowering soluble fiber. This ingredient also provides slow-release, low-glycemic carbs. Replacing part of the flour in recipes with oat bran is a good way to lower the glycemic index of baked goods. When using oat bran in recipes, choose a soft-textured brand like Quaker Oat Bran.

Oat Flour

Ground from whole-grain oats, oat flour lends a slightly sweet flavor and a tender texture to baked goods, reducing the need for both fat and sugar. Rich in fiber and nutrients, oat flour improves the nutritional profile of foods when you substitute it for part of the white flour in recipes. These qualities make oat flour a natural for healthy baking.

Oat flour can replace up to half of the flour in products like muffins, quick breads, cakes, and cookies. This product can be purchased in natural food stores and some grocery stores. Or make your own oat flour by grinding quick-cooking oats in a blender or food processor. One cup of oats will make about ¾ cup of flour.

Wheat Bran

A rich source of fiber, wheat bran is also loaded with B vitamins, magnesium, manganese, and selenium. Replacing part of the white flour with wheat bran is a good way to create hearty and nutritious quick breads and muffins.

Wheat Germ

Loaded with vitamin E, minerals, and B vitamins, this ingredient adds crunch and nutty flavor to baked goods. You can replace part of the flour in piecrusts, crumb toppings, cookies, quick breads, and other baked goods with this supernutritious product.

Whole-Wheat Pastry Flour

Made especially for products like quick breads, cookies, and cakes, this product has a lightly sweet flavor and softer texture than regular whole-wheat flour. Look for whole-wheat pastry flour (sometimes labeled "whole-grain" pastry flour) in natural foods stores and some grocery stores.

CALORIC SWEETENERS

Anyone who has tried to eliminate all of the sugar from a cookie, cake, or quick bread recipe understands the value of sugar in baked goods. Sugar makes baked goods moist and tender, provides bulk, and promotes browning during baking. Leave out too much sugar and you may end up with a product that is tough, dry, smaller in size, and just plain unappetizing! As discussed earlier in this chapter, some sugar is allowable in a diabetic diet as long as total carbs are kept under control. The recipes in this book will help you keep dietary sugar within healthy limits.

Are some sweeteners better choices than others? A variety of alternatives to white sugar—such as brown sugar, molasses, maple syrup, and honey—are widely available in grocery stores. Most health-food stores also sell unrefined sugar cane sweeteners, turbinado (raw sugar), and various types of fruit sweeteners. Many of these products do provide some nutrients including calcium, iron, magnesium, and potassium. In comparison, white table sugar contains no nutrients at all. Realize though, that the nutritional value of most sweeteners is still relatively small compared to that of more nutrient-dense foods like vegetable and fruits. The table below compares the nutritional content of some commonly available sweeteners.

Feel free to substitute your choice of sweeteners for sugar in any of the recipes in this book. Just keep in mind that you will usually get the best results when you substitute other granular sweeteners for sugar. Liquid sweeteners like honey, molasses, and maple syrup can be freely substituted for one another in recipes. If you want to replace sugar in a recipe with a liquid sweetener, you may have to reduce some of the liquid in the recipe slightly to compensate.

Fructose

Myths abound regarding the use of fructose in the diabetic diet, so this sweetener deserves special mention. Made from cornstarch, this granular sweetener looks like white table sugar and is about 1½ times sweeter. It is often sold alongside artificial sweeteners as an alternative for people with diabetes. High-fructose corn syrup is also used to sweeten sodas and many other processed foods.

Fructose is very slowly absorbed and produces a much lower blood glucose response than regular sugar does. Despite this, fructose is not recommended in large amounts because it is readily converted into fat and can raise blood triglyceride levels and increase the risk for heart disease. Eating too much fructose can also have a laxa-

SWEETENER (¼ CUP)	CALORIES	CARBS (GRAMS)	CALCIUM (MG)	IRON (MG)	MAGNESIUM (MG)	POTASSIUM (MG)
White sugar	194	50	0	0	0	0
Brown sugar	206	53	47	1	16	190
Turbinado (raw) sugar	183	47	41	1	14	169
Honey	257	70	5	0.4	2	44
Maple syrup	210	54	54	1	11	163
Molasses, light	206	53	135	3	199	752

tive effect in some people. And, like white table sugar, fructose is a highly refined sweetener and provides no nutrients.

What about the fructose that occurs naturally in fruits? Compared to sweets and desserts, fruits are much lower in carbohydrate content. For instance, a medium apple contains about 20 grams of carbohydrate. A piece of sugar-sweetened apple pie contains nearly three times this amount. Fruits also provide fiber and an arsenal of disease-fighting nutrients, making them a wholesome way to satisfy a sweet tooth.

Sugar Alcohols

Sugar alcohols are widely used in commercial "sugar-free" treats, so they also deserve special mention. Perhaps the best-known sugar alcohol is sorbitol. Maltitol, xylitol, isomalt, and hydrogenated starch hydrolysates are other examples of sugar alcohols commonly used in commercial foods.

Sugar alcohols are made from ingredients like beet sugar and cornstarch that have been chemically rearranged to resist digestion. As a result, sugar alcohols are poorly absorbed, have a minimal effect on blood sugar levels, and supply about half the calories of regular sugar. The caveat is, if too much is eaten, sugar alcohols can cause bloating, gas, and have a laxative effect. Like fructose and regular sugar, sugar alcohols are refined sweeteners and provide no nutrients.

SUGAR SUBSTITUTES

A variety of sweeteners are available today that supply few or no calories or carbohydrates. Many of these products can be used in cooking and baking, and recipes abound for "sugar-free" or "light" cookies, cakes, and other goodies. Just bear in mind that, as discussed earlier, replacing all of the real sugar in your own favorite recipes with a sugar substitute may produce disappointing results.

Do some recipes adapt better to using sugar substitutes than others? Definitely. Recipes like fruit pies and crisps, puddings, gelatin desserts, and fruit sauces can produce very good results with sugar substitutes. On the other hand, cakes, cookies, quick breads, muffins, and other flour-based baked goods will provide best results when only part of the sugar is replaced. See the latter part of this chapter (pages 27–31) for tips on slashing sugar in your favorite recipes. Here are some sugar substitutes that are commonly available.

Acesulfame-K

Sold under the brand name Sunette, acesulfame-K has a pleasant flavor and leaves no bitter aftertaste. This product is heat stable so can be used in cooked foods.

Aspartame

Also known as NutraSweet and Equal, Aspartame is made of two amino acids (the building blocks of proteins). It has a pleasant flavor and leaves no bitter aftertaste. Aspartame can be used in some cooked and baked recipes, but may lose its sweetness if cooked for too long or at too high temperatures. This is why it's best to add the sweetener at the end of the cooking process whenever possible.

One of the amino acids in aspartame, phenylalanine, must be avoided by people who have a genetic disorder known as phenylkenoturia (PKU). People who have this disorder cannot break down phenylalanine, so it accumulates in their blood, resulting in neurological problems. This is why aspartame-containing products are labeled with a warning to this effect.

Saccharin

For many years, saccharin (sold under the brand name Sweet'n Low) was sold with a warning that it caused cancer in laboratory animals. This warning was discontinued in the year 2000, the year the FDA determined saccharin to be safe for humans to consume. Saccharin is heat stable and may be used in cooking, but used in large amounts, it has a bitter aftertaste.

Sucralose

Sold under the brand name Splenda, this sweetener is made from sucrose in a process that substitutes chlorine atoms for part of the sugar molecule. It has a natural sugar taste and is heat stable, so can be used for cooking and baking. Of the sugar substitutes currently on the market, Sucralose is by far the best suited for cooking and baking. The recipes in this book were developed and tested using Splenda.

Stevia

This herbal sweetener has been used in South American for centuries. It has also been used in Japan since the early 1970s. Stevia has a slight licoricelike flavor that some people find overpowering. Since processing removes most of the flavor components, the more refined the stevia is, the less pronounced the licorice flavor will be.

While stevia has no known adverse effects, it has not undergone the scientific scrutiny that artificial sweeteners have, so the FDA has not yet approved it. This is why you won't find stevia sold alongside other sweeteners in your grocery store. You can, however, buy stevia in health-food stores, where it is sold as a dietary supplement. Realize that dietary supplements are not regulated as stringently as FDA-approved food ingredients and may have no guarantees of purity or long-term safety.

OTHER INGREDIENTS

Aside from the ingredients discussed so far, a few more items will prove useful as you prepare your diabetic dream desserts. Some ingredients may already be familiar to you, while others may become new and valuable additions to your pantry.

Cocoa Powder

This ingredient is a low-calorie way to add chocolate flavor to a variety of delicious desserts. For the deepest, darkest, richest cocoa flavor, use Dutch-processed cocoa in your chocolate treats. Dutching, a process that neutralizes the natural acidity in cocoa, results in a darker, sweeter, more mellow-flavored cocoa. Because of its smoother flavor, chocolate treats made with Dutch-processed cocoa can often be made with less sugar than those made with regular cocoa. Brands like Hershey's European-style cocoa are available in some grocery stores. Saco cocoa, a mixture of regular and Dutch-processed cocoa, is another good choice and is available in many stores.

Dried Fruits

A wide variety of dried fruits are available to add natural sweetness and interest to quick breads, cookies, and other treats. Dried apricots, cherries, cranberries, blueberries, plums, and dark and golden raisins are the most common examples. If you cannot find the type of dried fruit called for in a recipe, feel free to substitute another type, since all dried fruits contain a similar amount of carbohydrate on a cup-for-cup basis.

Fruit Juice Concentrates

Frozen fruit juice concentrates add natural sweetness and flavor to desserts, while adding nutrients like potassium and vitamin C. Juice concentrates contain about 25 to 40 percent less sugar than an equal amount of sugar, and a little bit can go a long way toward perking up the flavor of the recipe. Always keep cans of juices like orange, apple, and white grape juice concentrates in the freezer just for recipes. Besides being useful in their concentrated forms, these products come in handy when you need a small amount of juice for a recipe. By mixing 1 part juice concentrate with 3 parts water, you can quickly whip up some juice without having to purchase a large container of ready-made juice.

Sugar-free Gelatin Mixes

From mousses and fruit whips to pies and parfaits, sugar-free gelatin mixes can form the basis of many delicious low-carb desserts. Sweetened with calorie-free sugar substitutes, these products are considered a "free food" in diabetic diets.

Low-Sugar Jams and Fruit Spreads

Low-sugar jams and fruit spreads contain about half the calories and carbohydrate of regular spreads. "All-fruit" spreads are sweetened with fruit juice concentrates (usually white grape juice). The calories and carbs in all-fruit spreads are usually about the same as for regular spreads, so use them more moderately than the low-sugar spreads.

Sugar-free Strawberry Glaze

With 80 percent fewer carbohydrates and calories than sugar-sweetened glazes, ready-made sugar-free strawberry glaze is a convenient item for making glazed fruit pies and other fresh fruit desserts. Look for this product in the produce section of many grocery stores.

Nuts and Seeds

Although high in fat, nuts and seeds can and should be part of a healthy diet. The reason? These crunchy morsels contain heart-healthy, unsaturated fats and they supply protein, fiber, and a wide range of vitamins, minerals, phytochemicals, and antioxidants. All of these qualities help explain why nuts have been found to protect against heart disease, diabetes, and other health problems. If you are watching your weight you should be aware that nuts and seeds are high in calories. Just a quarter cup contains about 200 calories, so it's important to enjoy them in moderation.

Getting the Most Out of Nuts

To bring out the flavor of nuts, try toasting them. Toasting nuts intensifies their flavors and can transform a dish from ordinary into extraordinary. To toast nuts, simply arrange the desired amount in a single layer on a baking sheet and bake at 350 degrees until lightly browned with a toasted, nutty aroma. Chopped or sliced nuts will be done in as little as five minutes, while whole or halved nuts will take a few minutes longer. Just be careful to watch them closely during the last part of baking as they can become burned very quickly. To save time, toast a little extra and store leftovers in the freezer or refrigerator.

Low-Sugar Pie Fillings

Light (reduced-sugar) and no-added-sugar pie fillings such as cherry and apple are available in most grocery stores. These convenient products can star in a variety of dazzling dessert recipes.

Sugar-free Pudding Mixes

Available in both instant and cook-and-serve varieties, sugar-free pudding mixes are available in a wide variety of flavors. These products can help you create a variety of parfaits, mousses, pies, and other delectable desserts.

Spices and Flavorings

Ingredients like cinnamon, nutmeg, cardamom, orange and lemon rind, and vanilla extract add flavor and enhance the natural sweetness of recipes, reducing the need for sugar. Many herbs and spices have also been found to contain antioxidants, phytochemicals, and a variety of nutrients that offer unique health benefits, making them valuable additions to your diet.

Salt

By enhancing flavor, a little salt added to a cookie, cake, or dessert recipe can reduce the need for sugar. Salt is also a necessary ingredient in yeast breads, as it controls

Spice It Up!

If you love the spicy flavor of cinnamon, you may be interested to know that a dash of cinnamon just might be good medicine for diabetes. In a recent study, researchers found that people with type 2 diabetes who consumed 1 gram (about a half teaspoon) of cinnamon daily lowered their levels of blood sugar, cholesterol, and triglycerides by up to 30 percent over the forty-day study period. How does cinnamon work? Certain compounds in cinnamon are thought to boost the effectiveness of the body's own insulin and enhance the cells ability to process dietary sugars.

A word to the wise—while cinnamon can star in a variety of healthful treats, if you eat calories and carbs in excess of your daily needs, you will cancel out any benefits you receive. For some low-calorie ways to add cinnamon to your diet, add a dash to your morning coffee, tea, or oatmeal. But don't go overboard, as more is not always better. In fact, cinnamon contains some substances that can be toxic if eaten in large quantities. A half teaspoon per day is a safe and reasonable amount.

the rising of the yeast. For this reason, some of the recipes in this book call for a small amount of salt. However, with the exception of the yeast-risen dessert breads in chapter 8, any of the recipes in this book can be made with no salt at all. Another option is to switch to *light salt,* which was half the sodium of regular salt. Unlike regular salt, light salt is high in potassium, so should be avoided by people who need to restrict their potassium intake.

Cake Mixes

While cake mixes hardly qualify as "good carbs," they can serve as a starting point for a variety of quick-and-easy desserts. Chapter 2 will show you how to combine a convenient mix with low-sugar fillings and super-light frostings, to create simple desserts with a lot less carbohydrate and calories than a traditional made-from-mix cake.

Ladyfingers

These small finger-shaped sponge cakes can be used to create an array of easy and elegant pudding, ice-cream, and fruit desserts. Ladyfingers can be purchased in many bakeries and supermarkets.

Nonfat and Light Whipped Topping

Widely available in tubs in the freezer case of your grocery store, nonfat and light whipped toppings can be used to create creamy frostings, fillings, mousses, and other desserts. Try mixing in a little light vanilla yogurt to enhance the flavor and add an extra creamy texture. When you need just a decorative spritz of whipped cream, look for light whipped cream in pressurized cans in the dairy case.

Slashing Sugar in Dessert Recipes

When cutting back on the amount of sugar in dessert recipes, it's important to realize that sugar adds more than just sweetness. Understanding the various functions of sugar in cooking and baking will give you the edge when modifying your own favorite recipes and assure the best possible results. Besides adding sweetness, sugar:

- serves as a bulking agent to provide structure and volume to recipes
- adds tenderness to baked goods by inhibiting the development of *gluten,* a protein in wheat flour that forms tough strands during the mixing of batters
- caramelizes (turns an amber color) during baking, which promotes the browning of baked goods
- adds lightness to recipes when creamed with butter, margarine, or shortening
- absorbs water and helps retain moisture
- acts as a preservative to help retard spoilage
- promotes a smooth and stable consistency in baked custards and prevents the liquid from "weeping" out
- prevents the formation of large ice crystals and enhances the smoothness of ice cream and other frozen desserts

As you might guess, because sugar performs so many different roles in recipes, removing too much sugar can cause dramatic changes in the outcome. This is why sugar substitutes perform best in recipes where the main function of sugar is to provide sweetness. Fruit pie fillings, fruit crisps and cobblers, puddings, cheesecakes, and dessert sauces are examples of desserts that most easily adapt to using sugar substitutes. Recipes like cakes, quick breads, muffins, and cookies—which rely on sugar for volume, a tender texture, and browning—are much more difficult to make completely without sugar.

While slashing sugar in treats can often lead to disappointing results, if you know a few tricks of the trade, you can substantially cut sugar, carbs, and calories from many dessert recipes. Here are some tips for getting the best results.

CAKES

Sugar performs many vital roles in cakes by adding tenderness, moistness, volume, and browning. For this reason, replacing all of the sugar in cakes with a sugar substitute can cause your cake to turn out pale and dry with a rubbery texture—hardly a diabetic dream dessert!

Fortunately, some creative cooking techniques can help you slash sugar in cake batters by 30 to 50 percent. One of the best techniques is to substitute oat flour for up to half of the white flour. Oat flour has a slightly sweet flavor and produces a moist and tender texture, reducing the need for both sugar and fat. As a bonus, you also get a nutritional boost from incorporating oat flour into your product. Realize too that some cake recipes lend themselves better to cutting back on sugar than others. Recipes that include plenty of fruits and fruit purees (like a fresh pear or applesauce cake) as well as carrot cakes and chocolate cakes will adapt better to using sugar substitutes than will a plain white or yellow cake.

While you can trim a good bit of sugar from cake batters, frostings and fillings are where you can really slash sugar. Instead of gooey icings that may feature several cups of powdered sugar, choose low-sugar recipes made with ingredients like sugar-free puddings, light yogurt, light whipped toppings, and reduced-fat cream cheese (like the ones in chapter 2). This will dramatically lighten up your cake recipes. Alternatively, dust the top of cakes with just a few tablespoons of powdered sugar or spread with a thin layer of low-sugar fruit spread or preserves instead of topping with a thick frosting.

FRUIT PIES, CRISPS, AND COBBLERS

The fruit-filling portion of pies, crisps, and cobblers can often be made with no sugar at all, as sugar substitutes perform very well in these recipes. Fruit fillings may not be as thick and juicy though, since sugar lends a viscous quality. To compensate, you may need to add a few tablespoons of fruit juice and increase the amount of cornstarch or other thickening agent a bit. You can also enhance low-sugar fruit fillings by adding a bit of extra cinnamon, nutmeg, or other flavoring

As for crisp and cobbler toppings, they are not as adaptable to slashing sugar as the fillings are, since some sugar is necessary for structure, volume, texture, and browning. The best compromise is to cut back on or eliminate the sugar in the filling, replacing it with an equivalent amount of sugar substitute, but leave some sugar in the topping. The recipes in chapters 3 and 7 provide many examples of lower-sugar pies, crisps, and cobblers.

COOKIES

Of all recipes, cookies are the most difficult to make with less sugar, since sugar is a primary ingredient that gives cookies their structure and volume—not to mention the brown color, aroma, and texture that people expect from a really good cookie. Another problem is that when you cut back on sugar, you just end up with higher proportions of white flour and fat—two ingredients that should also be minimized in a healthy diet.

The best compromise is to leave in a moderate amount of sugar and focus on using more wholesome ingredients like oats, oat bran, and whole-wheat pastry flour instead of the nutrient-poor white flour used in traditional recipes. You can also use more healthful fats and oils and include nutritious ingredients like nuts and dried fruits in your cookie recipes. Meringue cookies are another good option, since they contain no flour at all and their light, airy texture provides volume with few calories and carbs. Chapter 5 presents plenty of ideas for delicious cookies that can fit into your diabetic diet.

Puddings and Custards

Many fabulous desserts such as trifles, mousses, and parfaits can be made using sugar-free pudding mixes. Made-from-scratch puddings and custards that are cooked on top of the stove can also easily be made with sugar substitutes instead of sugar. Baked custards are a little trickier, since sugar promotes a smooth and stable consistency in baked custards and prevents the liquid from "weeping" out once the custard has finished baking. Still, you can often cut the sugar in baked custards by half with excellent results. Add a little extra vanilla or dust the top with ground nutmeg to enhance sweetness and flavor.

Quick Breads

Like cakes, sugar performs many vital roles in quick breads by adding tenderness, moistness, volume, and browning. Still, you can often cut the sugar in quick breads by half with excellent results. To compensate for the lost flavor, you can add an equivalent amount of a sugar substitute. Adding a little extra vanilla or sweet spices like nutmeg, cardamom, cinnamon, or orange rind can also enhance sweetness.

One of the best ways to improve the texture in your low-sugar baked goods is to replace the white flour with whole-grain alternatives like whole-wheat pastry flour, oats, and oat flour. These ingredients will help maintain tenderness while providing a nutritional boost. Moreover, by choosing recipes that incorporate fruits and fruit purees you can create moist and delicious quick breads that need only a moderate amount of added sugar.

Frozen Desserts

Sugar substitutes can work well in homemade desserts such as granitas, ices, sorbets, frozen yogurt, and ice cream. However, since sugar prevents the formation of large ice crystals, your frozen dessert may not be as smooth and creamy as those made with large amounts of sugar. The difference in texture will be barely noticeable if the dessert is prepared in an ice-cream maker and eaten when freshly made. If you prepare the dessert in advance and freeze for several hours or more before eating it, ice crystals may form, causing a grainy texture.

Other Tips for Making Low-Sugar Treats

- Since sugar acts as a preservative to retard spoilage, low-sugar baked goods will last longer if stored in a refrigerator
- If your low-sugar baked goods do not brown enough to suit your taste, try using brown sugar (use light or dark brown sugar, depending on how much color and flavor you want) instead of white sugar. Or substitute a tablespoon of molasses for an equal amount of the sugar in the recipe. You can also add a few tablespoons of nonfat dry milk powder to cake, cookie, and quick bread recipes to promote browning.
- Low-sugar recipes may bake more quickly than those made with sugar, so check your low-sugar baked goods for doneness a few minutes before the end of the usual baking time.
- If your low-sugar baked goods do not rise as well as their high-sugar counterparts, try increasing the leavening (baking soda or baking powder) by 25 percent.

About the Nutrition Analysis

As these recipes were developed, every effort was made to keep calories under control. Carbs are kept at low to moderate levels and fats are used moderately with a focus on "good" fats. This allows you to enjoy a wide variety of tasty treats without blowing your calorie budget or sacrificing your future health.

The Food Processor nutrition analysis software (ESHA Research), along with product information from manufacturers, was used to calculate the nutrition information for the recipes in this book. For each recipe, information on calories, carbohydrate, dietary fiber, protein, fat, saturated fat, cholesterol, sodium, and calcium is provided. The serving size or unit upon which the nutrition analysis is based is clearly indicated for each recipe.

Sometimes recipes give options regarding ingredients. For instance, you might be able to choose between nonfat or reduced-fat cheese, eggs or egg substitute, or margarine or butter. This will help you create dishes that suit your tastes and your nutrition goals. Just bear in mind that the nutrition analysis is based on the first ingredient listed and does not include optional ingredients.

About the Diabetic Exchanges

In addition to the nutrition analysis, diabetic exchanges based on the Exchange Lists are provided for each recipe to assist people who use this meal-planning technique. The Exchange Lists are a meal-planning system that is sometimes used for devising diabetic and weight-loss diets. Foods that are similar in carbohydrate, protein, and fat content are grouped together into an "exchange list." Thus, any food on a list can be substituted or exchanged for another.

For all of the recipes in this book, diabetic exchanges are broken down into carbohydrate and fat exchanges, so you can easily exchange them for other carbohydrate foods such as starches, fruit, and milk in your diet. More information on using exchanges is available through your registered dietitian or diabetes educator.

2. Creative Cakes

A fresh-baked cake can add that special touch to many occasions. Unfortunately, cakes made with large amounts of white flour and sugar and slathered with sugary icing, top the list of high-carb desserts. Is there a way to create luscious cakes with fewer carbs and calories? Absolutely. The cakes in this chapter combine moderate amounts of sugar with low-cal sugar substitutes to keep carbs down. And light frostings or simple glazes replace gooey icings, saving even more carbs and calories.

But what about fat? With gobs of shortening and buttercream icings, cakes also top the list of high-fat desserts. Not these recipes. Low to moderate amounts of healthful oils and trans-free margarines add moistness and tenderness while keeping saturated fats to a minimum. Many of the delightful desserts in this chapter also feature wholesome whole-grain flours, fruits, and fruit purees. These healthful additions enhance flavor and texture, reducing the need for both fat and refined sugar.

So whether you are looking for a grand finale to an elegant meal or a fruit-filled coffee cake for a casual get-together, you need look no further. With a little creativity, you and your family will be delighted to find that sometimes you *can* have your cake and eat it, too.

Carrot-Spice Cake

YIELD: 20 SERVINGS

1 cup unbleached flour

1 cup oat flour

1¼ cups light brown sugar

Sugar substitute equal to ½ cup sugar

2 teaspoons ground cinnamon

½ teaspoon ground allspice

1½ teaspoons baking soda

¼ teaspoon salt

½ cup unsweetened applesauce

¾ cup fat-free egg substitute or 3 eggs,
   lightly beaten

½ cup canola oil

3 cups grated carrots (about 6 medium)

2 teaspoons vanilla extract

½ cup chopped walnuts

FROSTING

8-ounce block nonfat or reduced-fat cream
   cheese, softened to room temperature

Sugar substitute equal to ½ cup sugar

1 teaspoon vanilla extract

⅓ cup nonfat or light sour cream

1½ to 2 cups nonfat or light whipped
   topping

1. Preheat the oven to 350 degrees.
2. Place the flours, sugar, sugar substitute, cinnamon, allspice, baking soda, and salt in a large bowl and stir to mix well. Use the back of a spoon to press out the lumps in the baking soda. Add the applesauce, egg substitute or eggs, oil, carrots, and vanilla extract and stir to mix well. Fold in the walnuts.
3. Coat a 9-by-13-inch pan with nonstick cooking spray and spread the batter evenly in the pan. Bake for about 30 minutes, or until the top springs back when lightly touched and a wooden toothpick inserted in the center of the cake comes out clean. Remove the cake from the oven and cool to room temperature.
4. To make the frosting, place the cream cheese, sugar substitute, and vanilla in a medium bowl and beat with an electric mixer until smooth. Add the sour cream and beat to mix well. Add the whipped topping and beat just until mixed in.
5. Spread the frosting over the cake. Cover and refrigerate until ready to serve.

Nutritional Facts (per serving)

Calories: 194   *Carbohydrates:* 27g   *Cholesterol:* 1mg   *Fat:* 7.7g   *Sat Fat:* 0.5g

Fiber: 1.5g   *Protein:* 5g   *Sodium:* 200mg   *Calcium:* 64mg

Diabetic exchanges: 2 carbohydrate, 1½ fat

Variation

·······················

Pineapple Carrot Cake Substitute 8 ounces of crushed (undrained) pineapple for the applesauce. Substitute toasted pecans for the walnuts.

Nutritional Facts (per serving)

Calories: 200   *Carbohydrates:* 28g   *Cholesterol:* 1mg   *Fat:* 8g   *Sat Fat:* 0.6g

Fiber: 1.6g   *Protein:* 4.6g   *Sodium:* 200mg   *Calcium:* 63mg

Diabetic exchanges: 2 carbohydrate, 1½ fat

∴ Cherry Ripple Cake ∴

For variety, substitute chocolate cake mix and pudding mix for the vanilla.

YIELD: 20 SERVINGS

1 box (1 pound, 2.25 ounces) yellow cake mix

1 box (4-serving size) sugar-free instant vanilla pudding mix

¾ cup nonfat or light sour cream

½ cup water

¾ cup fat-free egg substitute

1⅓ cups no-added-sugar or light (reduced-sugar) cherry pie filling

GLAZE

⅓ cup powdered sugar

1½ teaspoons nonfat or low-fat milk

¼ teaspoon vanilla extract

2 tablespoons sliced almonds

1. Preheat the oven to 350 degrees.
2. Place the cake mix and pudding mix in a large bowl and stir to mix well. Add the sour cream, water, and egg substitute and beat with an electric mixer for 2 minutes. (The batter will be thick.)
3. Coat a 12-cup bundt pan with nonstick cooking spray and spread one-third of the batter evenly in the pan. Spoon half of the cherry pie filling in a ring over the center of the batter. Repeat the batter and filling layers, then finish off with the remaining batter.
4. Bake for about 40 minutes, or just until the top springs back when lightly touched and a wooden toothpick inserted on either side of the filling comes out clean.
5. Allow the cake to cool in the pan for 40 minutes, then invert onto a serving platter and cool to room temperature.
6. To make the glaze, combine the powdered sugar, milk, and vanilla extract in a microwave-safe bowl and stir to mix well. Microwave at high power for 20 seconds, or until hot and runny. Drizzle the hot glaze over the cake and sprinkle the almonds over the top. Let the cake sit for at least 15 minutes before slicing and serving.

Nutritional Facts (per serving)
Calories: 142   *Carbohydrates:* 27g   *Cholesterol:* 0mg   *Fat:* 2.6g   *Sat Fat:* 1g
Fiber: 0.6g   *Protein:* 2g   *Sodium:* 271mg   *Calcium:* 54mg
   Diabetic exchanges: 2 carbohydrate, ½ fat

Harvest Apple Cake

5 cups peeled and chopped apple (about
⅓-inch dice)

1 cup sugar

Sugar substitute equal to ½ cup sugar

½ cup dark raisins or chopped, pitted,
dried plums

1 cup unbleached flour

1 cup oat flour or whole-wheat pastry flour

2 teaspoons ground cinnamon

1 teaspoon baking soda

¼ teaspoon salt

¼ cup plus 2 tablespoons canola oil

½ cup fat-free egg substitute or 2 eggs,
beaten

2 teaspoons vanilla extract

½ cup chopped walnuts or toasted pecans
(page 25)

1. Place the apples, sugar, sugar substitute, and raisins in a medium bowl and stir to mix well. Set aside for 30 minutes.
2. Preheat the oven to 350 degrees.
3. Place the flours, cinnamon, baking soda, and salt in a large bowl and stir to mix well. Add the apple mixture, oil, egg substitute or eggs, and vanilla extract and stir to mix. Fold in the nuts.
4. Coat a 9-by-13-inch pan with cooking spray and spread the batter evenly in the pan. Bake for about 30 minutes or until the top springs back when lightly touched and a wooden toothpick inserted in the center of the cake comes out clean. Cool to room temperature before cutting into squares and serving.

Nutritional Facts (per serving)
Calories: 163 *Carbohydrates:* 25g *Cholesterol:* 0mg *Fat:* 6.2g *Sat Fat:* 0.4g
Fiber: 2g *Protein:* 2.8g *Sodium:* 100mg *Calcium:* 6mg
  Diabetic exchanges: 1½ carbohydrate, 1 fat

Fresh Pear Cake

½ cup unbleached flour

½ cup oat flour or whole-wheat pastry
    flour

⅔ cup sugar

Sugar substitute equal to ⅓ cup sugar

½ teaspoon baking soda

¼ teaspoon ground cardamom or nutmeg

¼ cup fat-free egg substitute or 1 egg,
    lightly beaten

3 tablespoons canola or walnut oil

2 tablespoons nonfat or low-fat milk

1 teaspoon vanilla extract

2½ cups sliced peeled fresh pears (about
    3 medium)

¼ cup golden or dark raisins or dried
    sweetened cranberries

¼ cup chopped walnuts or toasted pecans
    (optional)

1. Place the flours, sugar, sugar substitute, baking soda, and cardamom or nutmeg in a medium bowl and stir to mix well. Add the egg substitute or egg, oil, milk, and vanilla extract, and stir to mix. Fold in the pears, raisins or cranberries, and if desired, the nuts. Set the batter aside for 10 minutes and then stir for 10 seconds.

2. Coat an 8-by-8-inch pan with nonstick cooking spray and spread the batter evenly in the pan. Bake at 350 degrees for about 23 minutes or just until the top springs back when lightly touched and a wooden toothpick inserted in the center of the cake comes out clean. Serve warm or cool to room temperature before cutting into squares and serving.

Nutritional Facts (per serving)

Calories: 166   *Carbohydrates:* 28g   *Cholesterol:* 0mg   *Fat:* 4.9g   *Sat Fat:* 0.3g

Fiber: 1.5g   *Protein:* 2.4g   *Sodium:* 92mg   *Calcium:* 26mg

   Diabetic exchanges: 2 carbohydrate, 1 fat

Light Lemon Cake

1 box (1 pound, 2.25 ounces) white or lemon
   cake mix

1 cup water

½ cup nonfat or light sour cream

½ cup fat-free egg substitute

2 packages (4-serving size each) sugar-free
   lemon gelatin mix

1 cup boiling water

1 cup cold tap water

FROSTING

2 cups nonfat or light whipped topping

¾ cup light lemon yogurt

1. Preheat the oven to 350 degrees.
2. Place the cake mix, water, sour cream, and egg substitute in a large bowl and beat with an electric mixer for 2 minutes. Coat a 9-by-13-inch pan with cooking spray and spread the mixture evenly in the pan. Bake for about 30 minutes, or just until the top springs back when lightly touched and a wooden toothpick inserted in the center of the cake comes out clean. Let the cake cool to room temperature. Then, using a fork, poke holes in the cake at ½-inch intervals.
3. Place the gelatin mix in a medium bowl and add the boiling water. Whisk for 2 minutes or until the gelatin is completely dissolved. Stir in the cold water. Slowly pour the gelatin mixture over the cake, allowing it to be absorbed. Cover and refrigerate for at least 3 hours.
4. To make the frosting, place the whipped topping in a small bowl and fold in the yogurt. Spread the frosting over the cake and chill for an additional hour before serving.

Nutritional Facts (per serving)
Calories: 138   *Carbohydrates:* 26g   *Cholesterol:* 0mg   *Fat:* 2.3g   *Sat Fat:* 0.9g
Fiber: 0.2g   *Protein:* 3.1g   *Sodium:* 218mg   *Calcium:* 60mg
   Diabetic exchanges: 2 carbohydrate, ½ fat

Angel Pudding Cake

YIELD: 12 SERVINGS

2 cups nonfat or low-fat milk

1 box (4-serving size) sugar-free instant or cook-and-serve white chocolate pudding mix

1 angel food cake (about 14 ounces)

FROSTING

2 cups nonfat or light whipped topping

¼ cup plus 2 tablespoons light vanilla, strawberry, or raspberry yogurt

3 cups sliced fresh strawberries

1½ cups fresh raspberries

1. Use the milk to prepare the pudding according to package directions. (If using cook-and-serve pudding, chill for at least 1 hour before proceeding with the recipe.)

2. Using a serrated knife, cut a 1½-inch-deep channel in the top of the cake, leaving ⅜ inch of the cake intact on either side of the channel. (Reserve the cut-out cake for another use.) Place the cake on a 12-inch round serving platter and spoon the pudding evenly into the hollowed-out section of the cake.

3. To make the frosting, place the whipped topping in a medium bowl and fold in the yogurt. Spread the frosting over the sides and top of the cake, but do not cover the channel. Toss the berries together and arrange 1½ cups of the mixture over the top of the cake, covering the channel. Arrange the remaining fruit around the base of the cake. Chill for at least 2 hours before slicing and serving.

Nutritional Facts (per serving)

Calories: 136 *Carbohydrates:* 29g *Cholesterol:* 1mg *Fat:* 0.5g *Sat Fat:* 0.1g

Fiber: 2.4g *Protein:* 3.6g *Sodium:* 356mg *Calcium:* 107mg

Diabetic exchanges: 2 carbohydrate

Almond-Ricotta Cake Roll

YIELD: 12 SERVINGS

1 cup sliced almonds

⅔ cup sugar

½ cup unbleached flour

½ teaspoon baking powder

¼ teaspoon salt

4 eggs, separated

2 tablespoons orange juice

2 tablespoons instant sugar-free vanilla pudding mix

Sugar substitute equal to 2 tablespoons sugar

⅓ cup nonfat or low-fat milk

SAUCE

1½ cups Easy Apricot Sauce (page 54) or Really Raspberry Sauce (page 55)*

FILLING

15 ounces part-skim ricotta cheese

1. Preheat the oven to 350 degrees.
2. Place the almonds and half of the sugar in a food processor and process until the almonds are very finely ground. Transfer to a large bowl and stir in the flour, baking powder, and salt. Set aside.
3. Place the egg whites in a large bowl and beat with an electric mixer until foamy. Gradually beat in the remaining sugar, 1 tablespoon at a time, until stiff peaks form when the beaters are raised. Set aside.
4. Add the egg yolks and orange juice to the almond mixture and stir to mix well. Fold in about ⅓ of the whipped egg whites and then fold in the remaining whipped egg whites.
5. Line a 10-by-15-inch jelly-roll pan with waxed paper by laying a 16-inch piece of waxed paper in the pan and folding up the sides so that the paper covers the bottom and sides of the pan. Spread the batter evenly in the pan. Bake for about 10 minutes, or just until the cake springs back when lightly touched in the center.

*NOTE: You will need to make a double batch of sauce to have enough for this recipe.

6. While the cake is baking, lay a clean kitchen towel on a work surface. Remove the cake from the oven and immediately invert it onto the towel. Carefully peel off the waxed paper. Starting at the short end, roll the cake and towel up together. Place the cake roll on a wire rack and let cool to room temperature.

7. To make the filling, place the ricotta cheese, pudding mix, sugar substitute, and milk in a small bowl and beat with an electric mixer to mix well. Set aside.

8. Gently unroll the cooled cake just enough to allow the filling to be spread over the top. Spread the filling to within ½ inch of the outer edges. Roll the cake up and transfer to a serving plate. Cover and chill for at least 12 hours. Using a serrated knife, trim ½ inch from each end of the cake before slicing and serving. To serve, drizzle 2 tablespoons of the sauce over the bottom of a serving plate and top with a slice of cake.

Nutritional Facts (per serving)

Calories: 177   *Carbohydrates:* 20g   *Cholesterol:* 6.7mg   *Fat:* 7.6g   *Sat Fat:* 2.2g
Fiber: 1.4g   *Protein:* 8g   *Sodium:* 175mg   *Calcium:* 130mg
   Diabetic exchanges: 1 carbohydrate, 1 medium-fat meat, 1 fat

Peach Coffee Cake

YIELD: 8 SERVINGS

TOPPING
3 tablespoons chopped almonds or pecans

1 tablespoon sugar

CAKE
3 tablespoons margarine or butter

½ cup sugar

Sugar substitute equal to ¼ cup sugar

2 tablespoons fat-free egg substitute

1 teaspoon vanilla extract

¾ cup unbleached flour

1 teaspoon baking powder

*¼ cup plus 2 tablespoons nonfat or
   low-fat milk*

*1-pound can sliced peaches in juice,
   drained*

1. Preheat the oven to 350 degrees.
2. To make the topping, combine the nuts and sugar in a mini blender or food processor and process until the nuts are finely ground. Set aside.
3. Place the margarine, sugar, and sugar substitute in a medium bowl and beat to mix well. Beat in the egg substitute and vanilla. Combine the flour and baking powder and stir to mix. Add the flour mixture and the milk to the margarine mixture and beat just until well mixed.
4. Coat a 9-inch round cake pan with cooking spray and spread the batter evenly in the pan. Arrange the peach slices in concentric circles over the batter and sprinkle with the topping.
5. Bake for about 25 minutes, or until a wooden toothpick inserted in the center of the cake comes out clean. Let cool for at least 20 minutes. Serve warm or at room temperature.

Nutritional Facts (per serving)

Calories: 155   *Carbohydrates:* 27g   *Cholesterol:* 0mg   *Fat:* 4.5g   *Sat Fat:* 1g

Fiber: 1g   *Protein:* 2.6g   *Sodium:* 110mg   *Calcium:* 57mg

Diabetic exchanges: 2 carbohydrate, 1 fat

Zucchini Fudge Cake

YIELD: 20 SERVINGS

1 cup unbleached flour

1 cup oat flour

½ cup cocoa powder

1¼ cups sugar

Sugar substitute equal to ½ cup sugar

1¼ teaspoons baking soda

¼ teaspoon salt

1 teaspoon ground cinnamon

¾ cup room-temperature coffee

¼ cup plus 2 tablespoons fat-free egg substitute or 2 eggs, lightly beaten

½ cup canola oil

2 cups (moderately packed) grated zucchini (about 2 medium)

1 1/2 teaspoons vanilla extract

1/2 cup chopped toasted pecans (page 25) or walnuts

FROSTING

1 block (8 ounces) nonfat or reduced-fat cream cheese, softened to room temperature

Sugar substitute equal to 1/4 cup sugar

1/2 cup nonfat or low-fat milk

1 package (4-serving size) sugar-free instant white chocolate pudding mix

2 cups nonfat or light whipped topping

1. Preheat the oven to 325 degrees.

2. Place the flours, cocoa, sugar, sugar substitute, baking soda, salt, and cinnamon in a large bowl and stir to mix well. Add the coffee, egg substitute or eggs, oil, zucchini, and vanilla extract and stir to mix well. Fold in the nuts.

3. Coat a 9-by-13-inch pan with nonstick cooking spray and spread the batter evenly in the pan. Bake for 35 to 40 minutes, or just until the top springs back when lightly touched and a wooden toothpick inserted in the center of the cake comes out clean or coated with a few fudgy crumbs. Remove the cake from the oven and cool to room temperature.

4. To make the frosting, place the cream cheese and sugar substitute in a medium bowl and beat with an electric mixer until smooth. Slowly beat in the milk until the mixture is smooth. Add the pudding mix and beat for 1 minute to mix well. Add a little more milk if the mixture seems too thick. Add the whipped topping and beat just until it is mixed in.

5. Spread the frosting over the cake, cover, and refrigerate for at least 3 hours before cutting into squares and serving.

Nutritional Facts (per serving)

Calories: 184   *Carbohydrates:* 25g   *Cholesterol:* 1mg   *Fat:* 7.8g   *Sat Fat:* 0.7g
Fiber: 1.8g   *Protein:* 4.9g   *Sodium:* 255mg   *Calcium:* 46mg
   Diabetic exchanges: 1½ carbohydrate, 1½ fat

Moist Mocha-Fudge Cake

1 box (1 pound, 2.25 ounces) chocolate fudge
  cake mix

¾ teaspoon instant coffee granules

½ teaspoon ground cinnamon

20-ounce can no-added-sugar or light
  (reduced-sugar) apple pie filling,
  finely chopped

¼ cup plus 2 tablespoons fat-free egg
  substitute

½ cup chopped walnuts or chopped toasted
  pecans (page 25)

FROSTING

1¼ cups light vanilla yogurt

1 package (4-serving size) sugar-free instant
  white chocolate pudding mix

2 cups nonfat or light whipped topping

3 tablespoons chopped walnuts (optional)

1. Preheat the oven to 350 degrees.
2. Place the cake mix, coffee granules, and cinnamon in a large bowl and stir to mix well. Add the pie filling and egg substitute and stir with a wooden spoon to mix well. Fold in the walnuts. Coat a 9-by-13-inch pan with nonstick cooking spray and spread the batter evenly in the pan.
3. Bake for about 28 minutes, or just until the top springs back when lightly touched and a wooden toothpick inserted in the center of the cake comes out clean or coated with a few fudgy crumbs. Be careful not to overbake. Let the cake cool to room temperature.
4. To make the frosting, place the yogurt and pudding mix in a medium-sized bowl and beat with an electric mixer until smooth. Add the whipped topping and beat just until the topping is mixed in. Spread the frosting over the cooled cake and sprinkle the walnuts over the top if desired. Cover the cake and refrigerate for several hours before serving.

Nutritional Facts (per serving)
Calories: 161   *Carbohydrates:* 29g   *Cholesterol:* 0mg   *Fat:* 3.5g   *Sat Fat:* 0.7g
Fiber: 1.2g   *Protein:* 3.1g   *Sodium:* 302mg   *Calcium:* 52mg
  Diabetic exchanges: 2 carbohydrate, ½ fat

Glazed Mocha-Fudge Cake

YIELD: 20 SERVINGS

1¼ cups unbleached flour

¾ cup oat flour

½ cup cocoa powder (preferably Dutch-processed)

1 cup plus 2 tablespoons sugar

Sugar substitute equal to ½ cup sugar

1¼ teaspoons baking soda

½ teaspoon salt

1 cup nonfat or low-fat milk

¾ cup room temperature coffee

¼ cup plus 2 tablespoons canola oil

1 tablespoon white vinegar

1½ teaspoons vanilla extract

½ cup chopped walnuts or toasted pecans (page 25) (optional)

GLAZE

1 cup powdered sugar

2 tablespoons cocoa powder

1 tablespoon plus 2 teaspoons room temperature coffee

1 teaspoon vanilla extract

1. Preheat the oven to 350 degrees.
2. Place the flours, cocoa, sugar, sugar substitute, baking soda, and salt in a large bowl and stir with a wire whisk to mix well. Combine the milk, coffee, oil, vinegar, and vanilla extract in a bowl and mix well. Add the milk mixture to the flour mixture and whisk to mix well. Stir in the nuts if using.
3. Coat a 9-by-13-inch pan with cooking spray and spread the batter evenly in the pan. Bake for about 25 minutes, or until the top springs back when lightly touched and a wooden toothpick inserted in the center of the cake comes out clean.
4. To make the glaze, place all of the glaze ingredients in a small bowl and stir until smooth. Spread the glaze in a thin layer over the hot cake. Place the cake on a wire rack and let cool to room temperature before serving.

Nutritional Facts (per serving)

Calories: 154   *Carbohydrates:* 27g   *Cholesterol:* 0mg   *Fat:* 4.7g   *Sat Fat:* 0.5g

Fiber: 1.5g   *Protein:* 2.3g   *Sodium:* 144mg   *Calcium:* 21 mg

Diabetic exchanges: 2 carbohydrate, 1 fat

Fudge Cake with Raspberry Sauce

SAUCE

¼ cup white grape or orange juice

1½ cups frozen unsweetened raspberries

2 teaspoons cornstarch

Sugar substitute equal to 3 tablespoons sugar

CAKE

½ cup unbleached flour

½ cup oat flour

½ cup sugar

¼ cup cocoa powder (preferably Dutch-processed)

Sugar substitute equal to ⅓ cup sugar

½ teaspoon baking soda

¼ teaspoon salt

¾ cup water or room temperature coffee

3 tablespoons canola oil

1 teaspoon vanilla extract

1. To make the sauce, place the juice and raspberries in a 1-quart pot and place over medium heat. Cover and cook for several minutes or until the berries are thawed and begin to break down. Dissolve the cornstarch in a tablespoon of water and add to the pot. Cook for another minute or two, until the sauce thickens. Remove the pot from the heat and stir in the sugar substitute. Cover and chill until ready to serve.

2. Preheat the oven to 350 degrees.

3. To make the cake, place the flours, sugar, cocoa powder, sugar substitute, baking soda, and salt in a medium bowl and stir to mix well. Add the water or coffee, oil, and vanilla and stir with a wire whisk until smooth.

4. Coat a 9-inch round pan with cooking spray and pour the batter into the pan. Bake for about 16 to 18 minutes, or until the top springs when lightly touched and a wooden toothpick inserted in the center of the cake comes out clean. Let the cake cool in the pan.

5. When ready to serve, cut the cake into 8 wedges and top each wedge with 2 tablespoons of the sauce. If desired, garnish each serving with some light whipped topping and a sprinkling of chopped walnuts or sliced almonds.

Nutritional Facts (per serving)

Calories: 166   *Carbohydrates:* 27g   *Cholesterol:* 0mg   *Fat:* 6g   *Sat Fat:* 0.6g

Fiber: 3.4g   *Protein:* 2.5g   *Sodium:* 152mg   *Calcium:* 14mg

Diabetic exchanges: 2 carbohydrate, 1 fat

Chocolate-Cream Cake Roll

YIELD: 12 SERVINGS

1 cup unbleached flour

¾ cup sugar

Sugar substitute equal to ⅓ cup sugar

½ cup cocoa powder (preferably Dutch-processed)

¾ teaspoon baking soda

¼ teaspoon salt

½ cup unsweetened applesauce

3 eggs, beaten

1 teaspoon vanilla extract

1½ tablespoons powdered sugar

1½ cups Really Raspberry Sauce (page 55) (optional)

FILLING

1 package (4-serving size) instant sugar-free white chocolate, dark chocolate, or pistachio pudding mix

1 cup nonfat or low-fat milk

1 cup nonfat or light whipped topping

1. Preheat the oven to 350 degrees.
2. Place the flour, sugar, sugar substitute, cocoa, baking soda, and salt in a medium bowl and stir to mix well. Add the applesauce, eggs, and vanilla extract and stir to mix well.
3. Line a 10-by-15-inch jelly-roll pan with waxed paper by laying a 16-inch piece of waxed paper in the pan and folding up the sides so that the paper covers the bottom and sides of the pan. Spread the batter evenly in the pan. Bake for about 10 minutes or just until the cake springs back when lightly touched in the center.
4. While the cake is baking, lay a clean kitchen towel out on a work surface and sift the powdered sugar over the towel. Remove the cake from the oven and immediately invert it onto the towel. Carefully peel off the waxed paper. Starting at the short end, roll the cake and towel up together. Place the cake roll on a wire rack and let cool to room temperature.

5. To make the filling, place the pudding mix and milk in a small bowl and whisk for a couple of minutes, or until thickened. Fold in the whipped topping and set aside.

6. Gently unroll the cooled cake just enough to allow the filling to be spread over the top. Spread the filling to within ½ inch of the outer edges. Roll the cake up and transfer to a serving plate. Cover and chill for at least 12 hours. Using a serrated knife, trim ½ inch from each end of the cake before slicing and serving. If desired, spread 2 tablespoons of Really Raspberry Sauce (you will need to double the recipe) over the bottom of each serving plate and top with a cake slice.

Nutritional Facts (per serving)
Calories: 130   *Carbohydrates:* 27g   *Cholesterol:* 43mg   *Fat:* 1.4g   *Sat Fat:* 0.5g
Fiber: 1.3g   *Protein:* 3.6g   *Sodium:* 267mg   *Calcium:* 36mg
Diabetic exchanges: 2 carbohydrate

∴ Black Forest Cake ∴

This cake is made in a flan or tiara pan. The bottom of the pan has a raised center that makes an ideal place to put the filling after the cake has been baked.

YIELD: 10 SERVINGS

⅔ cup unbleached flour

⅔ cup oat flour

⅓ cup Dutch-processed cocoa powder

½ cup sugar

Sugar substitute equal to ⅔ cup sugar

½ teaspoon baking soda

½ teaspoon baking powder

¼ teaspoon salt

1 cup water

¼ cup canola oil

¼ cup fat-free egg substitute or 1 egg, beaten

1 teaspoon vanilla extract

FILLING

1 package (4-serving size) sugar-free instant chocolate pudding mix

1 cup nonfat or low-fat milk

1¼ cups no-added-sugar or light (reduced-sugar) cherry pie filling

1. Place the flours, cocoa, sugar, sugar substitute, baking soda, baking powder, and salt in a bowl and stir to mix well. Add the water, oil, egg substitute or egg, and vanilla and stir with a wire whisk until smooth.

2. Coat a 10-inch flan pan (or a 10-inch cake pan) with nonstick cooking spray and pour the batter into the pan. Bake at 350 degrees for 12 minutes, or until the top springs back when lightly touched and a wooden toothpick inserted in the center of the cake comes out clean or coated with a few fudgy crumbs.

3. Let the cake cool to room temperature in the pan and then invert onto a serving platter.

4. To make the filling, place the pudding mix and milk in a bowl and beat for 1 minute. Fill the depression in the top of the cake with the pudding. (If using a regular cake pan, spread the filling over the top of the cake.) Spread the pie filling over the top. Chill for at least 1 hour before serving.

Nutritional Facts (per serving)
Calories: 189   *Carbohydrates:* 30g   *Cholesterol:* 0mg   *Fat:* 6.2g   *Sat Fat:* 0.6g
Fiber: 2.2g   *Protein:* 4g   *Sodium:* 209mg   *Calcium:* 53mg
   Diabetic exchanges: 2 carbohydrate, 1 fat

German Chocolate Delight

This cake is made in a flan or tiara pan. The bottom of the pan has a raised center that makes an ideal place to put the filling after the cake has been baked.

YIELD: 10 SERVINGS

⅔ cup unbleached flour

⅔ cup oat flour

⅓ cup Dutch-processed cocoa powder

½ cup light brown sugar

Sugar substitute equal to ⅔ cup sugar

½ teaspoon baking soda

½ teaspoon baking powder

⅛ teaspoon salt

1 cup water

¼ cup canola oil

¼ cup fat-free egg substitute or 1 egg, beaten

1 teaspoon vanilla extract

FILLING

1 package (4-serving size) sugar-free instant
   butterscotch pudding mix

1½ cups nonfat or low-fat milk

⅓ cup shredded sweetened coconut

⅓ cup chopped pecans

1. Preheat the oven to 350 degrees.
2. Place the flours, cocoa, sugar, sugar substitute, baking soda, baking powder, and salt in a bowl and stir to mix well. Use the back of a spoon to press out any lumps in the brown sugar. Add the water, oil, egg substitute or egg, and vanilla and stir with a wire whisk until smooth.
3. Coat a 10-inch flan pan (or a 10-inch cake pan) with nonstick cooking spray and pour the batter into the pan. Bake for 12 to 15 minutes, or until the top springs back when lightly touched and a wooden toothpick inserted in the center of the cake comes out clean or coated with a few fudgy crumbs.
4. Let the cake cool to room temperature in the pan and then invert onto a serving platter.
5. To make the filling, place the pudding mix and milk in a bowl and whisk for 2 minutes, or until thickened. Stir in the coconut and pecans. Fill the depression in the top of the cake with the pudding mixture. (If using a regular cake pan, spread the filling over the top of the cake.) Chill for at least 1 hour before serving.

Nutritional Facts (per serving)

Calories: 224   *Carbohydrates:* 30g   *Cholesterol:* 0mg   *Fat:* 10g   *Sat Fat:* 1.8g
Fiber: 2.4g   *Protein:* 4.7g   *Sodium:* 332mg   *Calcium:* 67mg
   Diabetic exchanges: 2 carbohydrate, 2 fat

Mini Cherry Cheesecakes

12 reduced-fat vanilla wafers

1 cup nonfat or reduced-fat ricotta cheese

½ cup sugar

Sugar substitute equal to ½ cup sugar

1 tablespoon cornstarch

1½ teaspoons vanilla extract

1½ blocks reduced-fat (Neufchâtel) cream cheese

½ cup fat-free egg substitute

1 cup no-added-sugar or light (reduced-sugar) cherry pie filling

1. Preheat the oven to 325 degrees. Line 12 muffin cups with paper muffin liners and spray the liners with cooking spray. Place 1 vanilla wafer, flat side down, in the bottom of each cup.

2. Place the ricotta cheese, sugar, sugar substitute, cornstarch, and vanilla extract in the bowl of a food processor and process until smooth. Add the cream cheese and process until smooth. Add the egg substitute and process again.

3. Divide the filling among the muffin cups, spooning it over the vanilla wafers. Bake for about 25 minutes, or until the tops are no longer sticky to the touch. Let the cheesecakes cool in the pans for 20 minutes then transfer to wire racks to cool completely. Top each cheesecake with a rounded tablespoon of the cherry pie filling and refrigerate for at least 3 hours before serving.

Nutritional Facts (per serving)
Calories: 158   *Carbohydrates:* 16g   *Cholesterol:* 21mg   *Fat:* 6.4g   *Sat Fat:* 4g
Fiber: 0.2g   *Protein:* 7.6g   *Sodium:* 181mg   *Calcium:* 125mg
Diabetic exchanges: 1 carbohydrate, 1 fat

Blueberry Cheesecake

2 tablespoons graham cracker crumbs*

1 cup nonfat or reduced-fat ricotta cheese

½ cup sugar

Sugar substitute equal to ¾ cup sugar

1½ teaspoons vanilla extract

3 blocks (8 ounces each) light (Neufchâtel)
   cream cheese, softened to room
   temperature

1 tablespoon lemon juice

1 tablespoon cornstarch

½ cup fat-free egg substitute or 2 eggs

2 egg whites

TOPPING

3 cups fresh or frozen (unthawed)
   blueberries (about 12 ounces)

2 tablespoons orange juice

1 tablespoon cornstarch

Sugar substitute equal to ¼ to
   ⅓ cup sugar

1. Preheat the oven to 325 degrees. Coat a 9-inch springform pan with cooking spray and sprinkle the graham cracker crumbs over the bottom of the pan. Tilt the pan so the crumbs coat the bottom and 1 inch up the sides of the pan. Set aside.

2. Place the ricotta, ¼ cup of the sugar, all of the sugar substitute, and the vanilla in a large bowl and beat to mix well. Add the cream cheese and lemon juice and beat until smooth. Sprinkle the cornstarch over the top and beat to mix well.

3. Add the egg substitute or eggs to the cream cheese mixture and beat to mix well. Place the egg whites in a medium bowl. Wash off the beaters and then beat the egg whites until soft peaks form. Slowly add the remaining ¼ cup of sugar and beat until stiff peaks form when the beaters are raised. Fold half of the whipped egg whites into the cheesecake batter, then fold in the remaining whipped egg whites.

4. Spread the batter evenly in the prepared pan. Wrap a piece of heavy-duty aluminum foil over the bottom and up the sides of the pan (to prevent any leaks).

*If you prefer a more substantial crust, prepare Graham Cracker Piecrust (page 57) and pat it over the bottom and 1 inch up the sides of the pan. Bake at 350 degrees for 8 minutes, then let cool to room temperature before proceeding with the recipe.

Bake for about 55 minutes, or just until the center feels firm to the touch. Let the cake cool to room temperature.

5. To make the topping, place the blueberries and 1 tablespoon of the orange juice in a 2-quart pot. Cover and cook over medium heat for about 5 to 7 minutes, or until the berries soften and release their juices. Dissolve the cornstarch into the remaining orange juice. Stir the cornstarch mixture and the sugar substitute into the berry mixture and cook for another minute, or until the mixture thickens. Let cool to room temperature.

6. Spread the topping over the cake and chill for 8 hours or overnight before serving.

Nutritional Facts (per serving)
Calories: 232   *Carbohydrates:* 18g   *Cholesterol:* 41mg   *Fat:* 12g   *Sat Fat:* 8g
Fiber: 0.8g   *Protein:* 11g   *Sodium:* 303mg   *Calcium:* 147mg
  Diabetic exchanges: 1 carbohydrate, 2 fat

Easy Apricot Sauce

YIELD: ABOUT 1 CUP

15-ounce can apricots packed in juice
Sugar substitute equal to 2 to 3 tablespoons sugar

¼ cup juice from the canned apricots (or 2 tablespoons juice plus 2 tablespoons apricot brandy)

1. Drain the apricots, reserving the juice. Place the apricots, sugar substitute, and juice (or juice plus brandy) in a blender and blend until smooth.

2. Cover and chill until ready to serve.

Nutritional Facts (per 2-tablespoon serving)
Calories: 11   *Carbohydrates:* 3g   *Cholesterol:* 0mg   *Fat:* 0g   *Sat Fat:* 0g
Fiber: 0.4g   *Protein:* 0.3g   *Sodium:* 3mg   *Calcium:* 3mg
  Diabetic exchanges: ⅕ carbohydrate

Really Raspberry Sauce

YIELD: ABOUT 1 CUP

3 cups fresh or frozen (thawed) raspberries

Sugar substitute equal to ¼ cup sugar

1 tablespoon plus 1 teaspoon sugar

1½ tablespoons orange or white grape juice or raspberry liqueur

1. Place the raspberries in a blender or food processor. Add the sugar substitute, sugar, and juice or liqueur and puree until smooth.
2. Pour the mixture into a wire strainer and, using the back of a spoon, push the mixture through the strainer and into a bowl. Discard the seeds. Transfer the sauce to a covered container and chill until ready to use.

Nutritional Facts (per 2-tablespoon serving)
Calories: 22   *Carbohydrates:* 4.5g   *Cholesterol:* 0mg   *Fat:* 0g   *Sat Fat:* 0g   *Fiber:* 1g
Protein: 0.3g   *Sodium:* 1mg   *Calcium:* 5mg
Diabetic exchanges: ⅓ carbohydrate

3. Pleasing Pies, Tarts, and Pastries

laky and delicious, pies, tarts, and pastries are always a welcome treat. And whether made with a juicy fruit filling or a creamy custard filling, these goodies can be easily prepared with a lot less sugar and fat. In fact, most of the recipes in this chapter contain 50 to 75 percent less sugar than traditional recipes. Sugar substitutes and ingredients like sugar-free pudding mixes are used whenever possible to keep carbs under control. Low to moderate amounts of sugar are used where necessary to produce a pleasing texture and the right balance of sweetness, but without a sugar overload. Spices like cinnamon and nutmeg enhance the natural sweetness of recipes and wholesome whole grains are featured in many recipes to boost fiber and nutritional value. Fat is also kept at low to moderate levels, with an emphasis on healthful fats like canola oil, trans-free margarine, and various kinds of nuts.

So take out your pie and tart pans and get ready to enjoy a galaxy of homemade goodies. Lusciously sweet and meltingly tender, these are desserts that you will find yourself making time and time again.

Graham Cracker Piecrust

¾ cup finely ground graham cracker crumbs

½ cup toasted wheat germ

2 tablespoons sugar

Sugar substitute equal to 3 tablespoons sugar

3 tablespoons melted margarine or butter

1 tablespoon fat-free egg substitute

1. Preheat the oven to 350 degrees.
2. Place the graham cracker crumbs, wheat germ, sugar, and sugar substitute in a food processor and process for about 15 seconds to mix well. Add the margarine or butter and the egg substitute and process, pulsing for a few seconds at a time, until the mixture is moist and crumbly and holds together when pinched. Add a little more egg substitute if the mixture seems too dry.
3. Coat a 9-inch pie pan with nonstick cooking spray and press the mixture firmly over the bottom and sides of the pan. Bake for about 8 minutes, or until lightly browned. Let cool to room temperature before filling.

Nutritional Facts (per serving)

Calories: 127   *Carbohydrates:* 16g   *Cholesterol:* 0mg   *Fat:* 6.2g   *Sat Fat:* 1g
Fiber: 1.2g   *Protein:* 3g   *Sodium:* 130mg   *Calcium:* 8mg
   Diabetic exchanges: 1 carbohydrate, 1 fat

Chocolate-Almond Piecrust

YIELD: 8 SERVINGS

½ cup sliced almonds

2 tablespoons sugar

¾ cup chocolate graham cracker crumbs

Sugar substitute equal to 3 tablespoons sugar

1½ tablespoons melted margarine or butter

1½ teaspoons fat-free egg substitute

1. Preheat the oven to 350 degrees.
2. Place the almonds and sugar in a food processor and process until the almonds are finely ground. Add the graham cracker crumbs and sugar substitute and process to mix well. Add the margarine or butter and the egg substitute and process, pulsing for a few seconds at a time, until the mixture is moistened.
3. Coat a 9-inch pie pan with nonstick cooking spray and press the mixture firmly over the bottom and sides of the pan. (Place your hand inside a small plastic bag as you press to prevent sticking.)
4. Bake for about 8 minutes or until lightly browned. Let cool to room temperature before filling.

Nutritional Facts (per serving)

Calories: 109   *Carbohydrates:* 13g   *Cholesterol:* 0mg   *Fat:* 5.8g   *Sat Fat:* 0.9g

Fiber: 1g   *Protein:* 2.1g   *Sodium:* 89mg   *Calcium:* 18mg

Diabetic exchanges: 1 carbohydrate, 1 fat

∴ Nutty Piecrust ∴

YIELD: 8 SERVINGS

Unbleached flour (about 1 tablespoon)

1¼ cups sliced almonds or chopped hazelnuts

2 tablespoons sugar

Sugar substitute equal to 2 tablespoons sugar

Pinch salt

1½ teaspoons fat-free egg substitute

1. Preheat the oven to 350 degrees.
2. To make the crust, line a 9-inch pie pan with heavy-duty aluminum foil and spray with cooking spray. Lightly dust with the flour, shaking out the excess. Set aside.
3. Place the nuts, sugar, sugar substitute, and salt in a food processor and process until finely ground. Add the egg substitute and process for a few seconds more or until the mixture is moist and crumbly and holds together when pinched.
4. Press the nut mixture over the bottom and sides of the pan. (Place your hand inside

a small plastic bag as you press to prevent sticking.) Bake for about 8 minutes, or until the crust feels firm and dry and is lightly browned. Cool to room temperature, then peel away and discard the aluminum foil. Place the crust back in the pan. (Note: You can make the crust the day before and cover with foil until ready to use.)

Nutritional Facts (per serving)
Calories: 98   *Carbohydrates:* 6g   *Cholesterol:* 0mg   *Fat:* 7.5g   *Sat Fat:* 0.6g
Fiber: 1.8g   *Protein:* 3.3g   *Sodium:* 20mg   *Calcium:* 37mg
   Diabetic exchanges: ½ carbohydrate, 1½ fat

∴ *Pat-in Piecrust* ∴

YIELD: 8 SERVINGS

½ cup plus 2 tablespoons quick-cooking   *⅛ teaspoon salt*
   (1-minute) oats   *3 to 4 tablespoons canola oil*
½ cup plus 2 tablespoon unbleached flour   *1 tablespoon nonfat or low-fat milk*

1. Place the oats, flour, and salt in a medium bowl and stir to mix well. Add the oil and milk and stir until the mixture is moist and crumbly and holds together when pinched. Add a little more milk if needed.

2. Coat a 9-inch pie pan with cooking spray. Press the dough in a thin layer over the sides and bottom of the pan, forming an even crust.

3. For a prebaked crust, prick the crust with a fork at 1-inch intervals and bake at 400 degrees for about 12 minutes, or until lightly browned. Allow the crust to cool to room temperature before filling. When a prebaked crust is not desired, simply fill and bake the crust as directed in the recipe.

Nutritional Facts (per serving)
Calories: 101   *Carbohydrates:* 11g   *Cholesterol:* 0mg   *Fat:* 5.5g   *Sat Fat:* 0.4g
Fiber: 0.9g   *Protein:* 2g   *Sodium:* 37mg   *Calcium:* 6mg
   Diabetic exchanges: 1 carbohydrate, 1 fat

∴ Coconut-Oat Piecrust ∴

2½ cups oat-flakes-with-almonds cereal

¼ cup shredded sweetened coconut

2 tablespoons soft margarine

1½ teaspoons fat-free egg substitute

1. Preheat the oven to 350 degrees.
2. Place the cereal in a food processor and process until finely ground. There should be 1⅛ cups of crumbs. (Adjust the amount if necessary.) Add the coconut and process for 10 seconds more. Add the margarine and egg substitute and process, pulsing for a few seconds at a time, until the mixture is moist and crumbly and holds together when pinched. Add a little more egg substitute if the mixture seems too dry.
3. Coat a 9-inch pie pan with nonstick cooking spray and press the mixture firmly over the bottom and sides of the pan. Bake for about 8 minutes, or until lightly browned. Let cool to room temperature before filling.

Nutritional Facts (per serving)
Calories: 103   *Carbohydrates:* 15g   *Cholesterol:* 0mg   *Fat:* 4.7g   *Sat Fat:* 1.7g
Fiber: 1.5g   *Protein:* 2g   *Sodium:* 110mg   *Calcium:* 12mg
   Diabetic exchanges: 1 carbohydrate, 1 fat

60 · *Diabetic Dream Desserts*

Phyllo Tart Shells

YIELD: 6 SERVINGS

1 tablespoon plus 1 teaspoon sugar

¼ teaspoon dried grated lemon rind

4 sheets (about 14 by 18 inches) phyllo pastry (about 3½ ounces)*

Butter-flavored cooking spray

1. Preheat the oven to 350 degrees. Combine the sugar and lemon rind in a small dish and stir to mix. Set aside.

2. Spread the phyllo on a clean dry surface. Remove 1 sheet of phyllo and lay it on a clean, dry surface. Spray the sheet lightly with the cooking spray and sprinkle with 1 teaspoon of the sugar mixture. Top with another phyllo sheet, spray with cooking spray, and sprinkle with the sugar mixture. Repeat with the remaining 2 sheets.

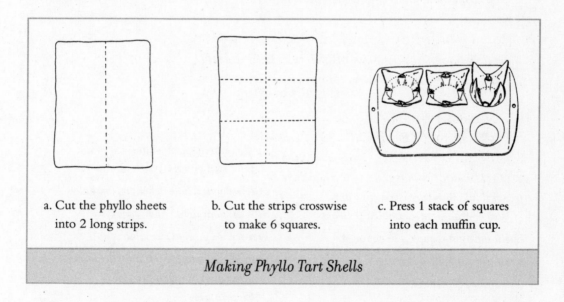

a. Cut the phyllo sheets into 2 long strips.

b. Cut the strips crosswise to make 6 squares.

c. Press 1 stack of squares into each muffin cup.

Making Phyllo Tart Shells

*When working with phyllo, be sure to cover it with a damp towel (to prevent it from drying out) as you work. Remove sheets as you need them, being sure to re-cover the remaining dough.

3. Cut the stack of phyllo sheets lengthwise into two 18-inch-long strips. Then cut each strip crosswise to make 3 pieces, each about 6 by 7 inches. You should now have 6 stacks of phyllo squares, each 4 layers thick. Turn the edges of each phyllo sheet slightly so that the corners of each are staggered.

4. Coat 6 jumbo muffin cups or custard cups with cooking spray. Gently press 1 stack of phyllo squares into each cup, pleating as necessary, to make it fit. Press the corners back slightly.

5. Bake for about 8 minutes, or until light golden brown. Let the shells cool for 5 minutes then transfer to wire racks to cool completely. The shells can be stored in an airtight container for several days before using.

Nutritional Facts (per serving)

Calories: 62 *Carbohydrates:* 11g *Cholesterol:* 0mg *Fat:* 1.2g *Sat Fat:* 0.2g
Fiber: 0.3g *Protein:* 1g *Sodium:* 80mg *Calcium:* 2mg
  Diabetic exchanges: 1 carbohydrate

Apple Crumb Pie

YIELD: 8 SERVINGS

1 unbaked Pat-in Piecrust (page 59)

FILLING

6 cups thinly sliced peeled cooking apples
  such as Fuji, Gala, or Golden Delicious

Sugar substitute equal to ½ cup sugar

2 tablespoons light brown sugar

2 teaspoons cornstarch

¼ teaspoon ground cinnamon

¼ teaspoon ground nutmeg

TOPPING

⅓ to ½ cup chopped walnuts
  or toasted pecans (page 25)

3 tablespoons whole-wheat pastry flour

3 tablespoons light brown sugar

¾ teaspoon ground cinnamon

1 tablespoon reduced-fat margarine or
  light butter, brought to room
  temperature

1. Preheat the oven to 400 degrees.
2. To make the filling, combine all of the filling ingredients in a large bowl and toss to mix well.
3. To make the topping, combine the nuts, flour, sugar, and cinnamon and stir to mix. Add the margarine or butter and stir until the mixture is moist and crumbly. Set aside.
4. Pile the filling into the crust and cover the pie loosely with a piece of aluminum foil. Bake for 20 minutes. Sprinkle the topping evenly over the filling. Reduce the oven temperature to 375 degrees and bake uncovered for an additional 30 minutes, or until the filling is tender and the topping is golden brown.
5. Let the pie cool for at least 30 minutes before serving.

Nutritional Facts (per serving)
Calories: 229   *Carbohydrates:* 34g   *Cholesterol:* 0mg   *Fat:* 9.3g   *Sat Fat:* 0.8g
Fiber: 3g   *Protein:* 3.8g   *Sodium:* 52mg   *Calcium:* 16mg
   Diabetic exchanges: 2 carbohydrate, 2 fat

Sour Cream Apple Pie

YIELD: 8 SERVINGS

1 unbaked Pat-in Piecrust (page 59)

4 cups thinly sliced peeled cooking apples such as Fuji, Gala, or Golden Delicious

FILLING
1 cup nonfat or light sour cream
¼ cup fat-free egg substitute
Sugar substitute equal to ½ cup sugar
2 tablespoons sugar
1 tablespoon cornstarch
¾ teaspoon vanilla extract

TOPPING
⅓ chopped walnuts
3 tablespoons whole-wheat pastry flour
3 tablespoons light brown sugar
½ teaspoon ground cinnamon
1 tablespoon reduced-fat margarine or light butter, brought to room temperature

1. Preheat the oven to 400 degrees.
2. To make the filling, combine all of the filling ingredients except for the apples and whisk to mix well. Stir in the apples.
3. To make the topping, combine the walnuts, flour, sugar, and cinnamon and stir to mix. Add the margarine or butter and stir until the mixture is moist and crumbly. Set aside.
4. Pile the filling into the crust and cover the pie loosely with a piece of aluminum foil. Bake for 25 minutes or until the filling begins to set around the edges. Sprinkle the topping evenly over the filling. Reduce the oven temperature to 375 degrees and bake uncovered for an additional 20 minutes, or until the filling is tender and the topping is golden brown. Cover the pie loosely with foil during the last few minutes of baking if the topping starts to brown too quickly.
5. Let the pie cool for at least 1 hour before serving. Refrigerate leftovers.

Nutritional Facts (per serving)
Calories: 250   *Carbohydrates:* 35g   *Cholesterol:* 0mg   *Fat:* 9.5g   *Sat Fat:* 1g
Fiber: 2.6g   *Protein:* 6g   *Sodium:* 89mg   *Calcium:* 56mg
Diabetic exchanges: 2 carbohydrate, 2 fat

Maple Pear Pie

YIELD: 8 SERVINGS

6 cups sliced, peeled fresh pears

Sugar substitute equal to ⅓ cup sugar

1 tablespoon plus 1 teaspoon cornstarch

½ teaspoon ground cinnamon

½ teaspoon ground nutmeg

1 unbaked Pat-in Piecrust (page 59)

3 tablespoons maple syrup

1. Preheat the oven to 400 degrees.
2. Place the pears in a large bowl. Combine the sugar substitute, cornstarch, cinnamon, and nutmeg and stir to mix. Sprinkle the sugar substitute mixture over the pears and toss to mix well.

3. Arrange a layer of pear slices in a spiral pattern over the bottom of the crust. Continue building layers in this manner until all of the pear slices are used. Drizzle the maple syrup over the top.

4. Cover the pie loosely with aluminum foil and bake for 15 minutes. Reduce the heat to 375 degrees and bake for an additional 45 minutes, or until the edges are bubbly. Remove the foil during the last 10 minutes of baking. Let the pie cool for at least 1 hour before serving.

Nutritional Facts (per serving)
Calories: 199   *Carbohydrates:* 35g   *Cholesterol:* 0mg   *Fat:* 6g   *Sat Fat:* 0.5g
Fiber: 3.8g   *Protein:* 2.5g   *Sodium:* 2mg   *Calcium:* 24mg
Diabetic exchanges: 2 carbohydrate, 1 fat

Phyllo Peach Pie

For variety, substitute pears for the peaches and walnuts or pecans for the almonds.

YIELD: 8 SERVINGS

¼ cup sliced almonds

1½ tablespoons sugar

6 cups thinly sliced peeled fresh peaches

1½ tablespoons cornstarch

Sugar substitute equal to ⅓ cup sugar

¼ cup reduced-sugar apricot jam or fruit spread

*8 sheets (about 14 by 18 inches each) phyllo pastry (about 5 ounces)**

Butter-flavored cooking spray

1. Preheat the oven to 350 degrees.
2. Combine the almonds and sugar in a mini food processor or blender jar and process until finely ground. Set aside.

*When working with phyllo, be sure to cover it with a damp towel (to prevent it from drying out) as you work. Remove sheets as you need them, being sure to re-cover the remaining dough.

3. Combine the peaches, cornstarch, and sugar substitute and toss to mix. Add the apricot jam and toss again. Set aside.

4. Coat a 9-inch pie pan with cooking spray and lightly press one of the phyllo sheets into the pan, allowing the edges to hang over the side. Spray the sheet with cooking spray and sprinkle with 1½ teaspoons of the almond mixture. Repeat with the remaining phyllo sheets, rotating the pan about a quarter turn after you add each sheet, so that the sheets overlap.

5. Spread the peach mixture evenly in the pan and fold the phyllo in to cover the filling. Spray the top with cooking spray and sprinkle with the remaining almond mixture.

6. Using a serrated knife, score through the top crust to make 8 wedges. (This will prevent the crust from flaking excessively when the pie is cut into serving pieces.)

7. Bake for about 50 minutes, or until the fruit is tender and the top is golden brown. Cover loosely with foil during the last part of baking if the crust begins to brown too quickly. Let cool for at least 40 minutes before serving.

Nutritional Facts (per serving)
Calories: 166 *Carbohydrates:* 31g *Cholesterol:* 0mg *Fat:* 4.2g *Sat Fat:* 0.5g
Fiber: 3.3g *Protein:* 3g *Sodium:* 89mg *Calcium:* 17mg
Diabetic exchanges: 2 carbohydrate, 1 fat

Deep-Dish Pumpkin Pie

YIELD: 8 SERVINGS

1 unbaked Pat-in Piecrust (page 59)
  (pat into a 9-inch deep-dish pie pan)
1½ cups cooked mashed or canned pumpkin
¼ cup plus 2 tablespoons dark brown sugar
Sugar substitute equal to ½ cup sugar
2 to 2 ½ teaspoons pumpkin pie spice

1 teaspoon vanilla extract
⅛ teaspoon salt
12-ounce can evaporated fat-free or
  low-fat milk
½ cup fat-free egg substitute

1. Combine the pumpkin, brown sugar, sugar substitute, pie spice, vanilla, and salt and whisk to mix well. Whisk in the milk and egg substitute.
2. Pour the filling into the crust and bake uncovered at 400 degrees for 15 minutes. Reduce the oven temperature to 375 degrees and bake for an additional 40 minutes, or until a sharp knife inserted in the center of the pie comes out clean.
3. Let the pie cool to room temperature before serving. Refrigerate leftovers.

Nutritional Facts (per serving)
Calories: 190   *Carbohydrates:* 30g   *Cholesterol:* 2mg   *Fat:* 5.7g   *Sat Fat:* 0.6g
Fiber: 2.3g   *Protein:* 6g   *Sodium:* 129mg   *Calcium:* 153mg
Diabetic exchanges: 2 carbohydrate, 1 fat

Southern Sweet Potato Pie

YIELD: 8 SERVINGS

1 unbaked Pat-in Piecrust (page 59)

FILLING
*1 pound (about 2 medium) sweet potatoes or
1 can (1 pound) sweet potatoes, drained*
1 cup evaporated nonfat or low-fat milk
½ cup fat-free egg substitute

¼ cup dark brown sugar
Sugar substitute equal to ¼ cup sugar
2 teaspoons ground cinnamon
½ teaspoon ground nutmeg
Pinch salt
1 teaspoon vanilla extract

1. If using fresh sweet potatoes, place them on a baking sheet and bake at 400 degrees for about 50 minutes, or until tender. Let cool, then remove the peel and cut into 1-inch pieces.
2. Preheat the oven to 350 degrees.
3. Place all of the filling ingredients in a blender and blend until smooth. Pour the filling into the crust.
4. Bake for about 45 minutes, or until a sharp knife inserted near the center of the

pie comes out clean. Let the pie cool to room temperature before serving. Refrigerate leftovers.

Nutritional Facts (per serving)

Calories: 191   *Carbohydrates:* 29g   *Cholesterol:* 1mg   *Fat:* 5.6g   *Sat Fat:* 0.5g

Fiber: 1.5g   *Protein:* 6.5g   *Sodium:* 183mg   *Calcium:* 121mg

Diabetic exchanges: 2 carbohydrate, 1 fat

Banana Dream Pie

YIELD: 8 SERVINGS

1 package (6-serving size) sugar-free cook-and-serve vanilla pudding mix

2¾ cups nonfat or low-fat milk

1 prebaked Graham Cracker Piecrust (page 57) or Coconut-Oat Piecrust (page 60)

2 cups sliced bananas

TOPPING

1½ cups nonfat or light whipped topping

⅓ cup light vanilla yogurt

2 tablespoons sliced almonds or toasted shredded coconut (optional)

1. Place pudding mix in a 2-quart glass bowl and slowly whisk in the milk. Microwave at high power for about 8 minutes, stirring every couple of minutes until the pudding is thickened and bubbly. Let the pudding cool for 5 minutes, stirring twice.

2. Spread one-fourth of the pudding over the crust and arrange half of the bananas over the pudding in a single layer. Repeat the pudding and banana layers and finish off with the remaining pudding. Place the pie in the refrigerator and chill uncovered for 2 hours.

3. Fold the yogurt into the whipped topping and spread over the pie, swirling the top. Sprinkle the almonds or coconut over the top, if using. Cover and chill for an additional hour, or until the filling is set, before serving.

Nutritional Facts (per serving)

Calories: 189   *Carbohydrates:* 28g   *Cholesterol:* 2mg   *Fat:* 5.8g   *Sat Fat:* 1.3g
Fiber: 1.2g   *Protein:* 6.4g   *Sodium:* 244mg   *Calcium:* 127mg

   Diabetic exchanges: 2 carbohydrate, 1 fat

∴ Strawberry Chiffon Pie ∴

For variety, substitute frozen raspberries and raspberry gelatin for the strawberry.

YIELD: 8 SERVINGS

2 cups frozen strawberries

1 package (4-serving size) sugar-free strawberry gelatin

½ cup boiling water

½ cup nonfat or light sour cream

1½ to 2 cups nonfat or light whipped topping

1 prebaked Graham Cracker Piecrust (page 57) or Chocolate-Almond Piecrust (page 57)

1. Coarsely chop the strawberries, set aside to thaw, and then mash with a fork.
2. Place the gelatin in a large heatproof bowl and add the boiling water. Whisk for 2 minutes, or until the gelatin is completely dissolved. Set aside for 10 minutes to cool slightly. Whisk in first the sour cream and then the strawberries, along with the juices that have accumulated.
3. Place the gelatin mixture in the refrigerator for about 40 minutes, or until the consistency of pudding. Whisk the mixture well and then fold in the whipped topping.
4. Spoon the mixture into the pie shell and chill for several hours, or until set, before serving.

Nutritional Facts (per serving)

Calories: 173   *Carbohydrates:* 26g   *Cholesterol:* 0mg   *Fat:* 5.7g   *Sat Fat:* 1.2g
Fiber: 2g   *Protein:* 4.8g   *Sodium:* 152mg   *Calcium:* 30mg

   Diabetic exchanges: 2 carbohydrate, 1 fat

Summer Berry Pie

YIELD: 8 SERVINGS

1 Nutty Piecrust (page 58)

2½ cups fresh raspberries or sliced
   strawberries

1½ cups fresh blackberries or blueberries

1½ cups sugar-free strawberry glaze

1 cup nonfat or light whipped topping
   (optional)

1. Combine the berries and glaze in a large bowl and toss to mix.
2. Spread the berry mixture in the pie crust and chill for 1 hour before serving. Top each serving with some whipped topping if desired.

Nutritional Facts (per serving)
Calories: 141   *Carbohydrates:* 17g   *Cholesterol:* 0mg   *Fat:* 7.8g   *Sat Fat:* 0.6g
Fiber: 5.8g   *Protein:* 3.8g   *Sodium:* 79mg   *Calcium:* 54mg
Diabetic exchanges: 1 carbohydrate, 1½ fat

Fabulous Fruit Pie

YIELD: 8 SERVINGS

2 tablespoons cornstarch

Sugar substitute equal to 3 tablespoons
   sugar

¾ cup orange juice

8-ounce can crushed pineapple in juice

1 prebaked Coconut-Oat Piecrust (page 60)
   or Graham Cracker Piecrust (page 57)

1 cup sliced fresh strawberries

2 kiwi fruit, peeled and sliced
   ¼-inch thick

1 cup sliced bananas

5 strawberry slices (garnish)

1. Place the cornstarch, sugar substitute, and 3 tablespoons of the orange juice in a small pot and stir to mix well. Add the remaining orange juice and then the undrained pineapple. Cook and stir over medium heat until thickened and bubbly. Set aside to cool for 15 minutes.

2. Spread half of the pineapple mixture evenly over the crust. Arrange the strawberries in a circular pattern over the pineapple mixture. Arrange the kiwi slices and then the bananas over the strawberries. Top with the remaining pineapple mixture and garnish with the strawberry slices.

3. Chill the pie for several hours, or until set, before serving.

Nutritional Facts (per serving)
Calories: 173   *Carbohydrates:* 32g   *Cholesterol:* 0mg   *Fat:* 5g   *Sat Fat:* 1.8g
Fiber: 3.3g   *Protein:* 2.8g   *Sodium:* 113mg   *Calcium:* 27mg
Diabetic exchanges: 2 carbohydrate, 1 fat

Cappuccino Pie

YIELD: 8 SERVINGS

½ cup room temperature coffee

1 envelope (¼ ounce) unflavored gelatin

¼ cup coffee liqueur

1 cup nonfat or light ricotta cheese

Sugar substitute equal to ⅓ cup sugar

⅛ teaspoon ground cinnamon

2 cups nonfat or light whipped topping

1 Chocolate-Almond Piecrust (page 57)

1½ tablespoons shaved dark chocolate

1. Place 2 tablespoons of the coffee in a blender. Sprinkle the gelatin over the coffee and let sit for 2 minutes. Bring the remaining coffee to a boil and pour over the mixture in the blender. Blend for 1 minute, until the gelatin is completely dissolved. Set aside for 5 minutes to cool slightly.

2. Add the liqueur to the blender mixture and blend to mix. Add the ricotta, sugar substitute, and cinnamon and blend until smooth. Pour the mixture into a large

bowl and refrigerate for about 30 minutes, or until the consistency of pudding. Whisk until smooth and then fold in the whipped topping.

3. Spread the ricotta mixture into the piecrust, swirling the top. Sprinkle the chocolate over the top. Cover and chill for at least 3 hours, or until set.

Nutritional Facts (per serving)

Calories: 208   *Carbohydrates:* 27g   *Cholesterol:* 1mg   *Fat:* 7g   *Sat Fat:* 1.2g
Fiber: 1.1g   *Protein:* 7.2g   *Sodium:* 128mg   *Calcium:* 169mg
Diabetic exchanges: 2 carbohydrate, 1½ fat

∴ *Apricot-Custard Tart* ∴

YIELD: 8 SERVINGS

1 prebaked Graham Cracker Piecrust (page 57)*

FILLING
1¾ cups nonfat or low-fat milk
1 package (4-serving size) cook-and-serve sugar-free vanilla pudding mix

TOPPING
1-pound can apricot halves in juice
Sugar substitute equal to 2 tablespoons sugar
1 tablespoon cornstarch

1. Use the milk to prepare the pudding according to package directions. Let the pudding cool for 5 minutes, stirring twice. Pour into the pie shell and refrigerate for 1 hour.
2. Drain the apricot halves, reserving the juice and one of the apricot halves. Arrange the remaining apricot halves, cut side down on top of the pudding.
3. Place ½ cup of juice from the apricots, the remaining apricot half, the sugar substitute, and cornstarch in a blender and blend until smooth. Pour the mixture into a small pot and cook over medium heat, stirring frequently, until the mixture is

*When making the crust, press the mixture over the bottom and 1 inch up the sides of a 9-inch tart or springform pan.

thickened and bubbly. Set the mixture aside for 5 minutes to cool, then stir and drizzle over the tart, covering the apricot halves.

4. Refrigerate the tart for several hours or until set before serving.

Nutritional Facts (per serving)
Calories: 162   *Carbohydrates:* 24g   *Cholesterol:* 1mg   *Fat:* 5g   *Sat Fat:* 1.3g
Fiber: 1.7g   *Protein:* 5g   *Sodium:* 196mg   *Calcium:* 76mg
   Diabetic exchanges: 1½ carbohydrate, 1 fat

∴ Simply Strawberry Tarts ∴

For variety, substitute fresh raspberries, blackberries, or blueberries for part of the strawberries.

YIELD: 6 SERVINGS

4 cups fresh strawberry halves

1½ cups sugar-free strawberry glaze

6 Phyllo Tart Shells (page 61)

1. Place the berries and glaze in a medium bowl and toss to mix.
2. Divide the mixture between the tart shells and serve immediately.

Nutritional Facts (per serving)
Calories: 100   *Carbohydrates:* 22g   *Cholesterol:* 0mg   *Fat:* 1.4g   *Sat Fat:* 0.2g
Fiber: 2.6g   *Protein:* 1.6g   *Sodium:* 161mg   *Calcium:* 16mg
   Diabetic exchanges: 1½ carbohydrate

Lemon Fruit Tarts

YIELD: 6 SERVINGS

¾ cup Light Lemon Curd (below)

6 Phyllo Tart Shells (page 61)

2 cups mixed fresh berries

¾ cup nonfat or light whipped topping (optional)

1. Spoon 2 tablespoons of the lemon curd into each tart shell.
2. Spoon ⅓ cup of the fruit over the lemon curd in each shell. Top each dessert with some of the whipped topping if desired. Serve immediately.

Nutritional Facts (per serving)
Calories: 147   Carbohydrates: 32g   Cholesterol: 0mg   Fat: 1.9g   Sat Fat: 0.2g
Fiber: 3.5g   Protein: 2.3g   Sodium: 94mg   Calcium: 22mg
Diabetic exchanges: 2 carbohydrate

Light Lemon Curd

YIELD: 1⅛ CUPS

1½ tablespoons cornstarch

⅓ cup sugar

¾ cup orange juice

½ cup lemon juice

¼ cup fat-free egg substitute

Sugar substitute equal to ⅓ cup sugar

1. Place the cornstarch and sugar in a 1½-quart pot. Add 3 tablespoons of the orange juice and stir to dissolve the cornstarch. Stir in the remaining orange juice and the lemon juice. Place the pot over medium heat and cook, stirring constantly, until the mixture is thickened and bubbly.
2. Remove the pot from the heat. Place the egg substitute and sugar substitute in a

2-cup bowl and mix well. Slowly whisk ¼ cup of the hot juice mixture into the egg mixture. Then slowly whisk the egg mixture back into the pot.

3. Return the pot to medium heat and cook, whisking constantly, for another minute or two, or until the mixture is thickened and bubbly. Let the mixture cool to room temperature without stirring. Transfer to a covered container and chill until ready to use.

Nutritional Facts (per tablespoon)
Calories: 27   *Carbohydrates:* 6.5g   *Cholesterol:* 0mg   *Fat:* 0.2g   *Sat Fat:* 0g
Fiber: 0.1g   *Protein:* 0.4g   *Sodium:* 7mg   *Calcium:* 3mg
    Diabetic exchanges: ½ carbohydrate

∴ *Summer Fruit Tarts* ∴

YIELD: 6 SERVINGS

1¾ cups nonfat or low-fat milk

1 package (4-serving size) sugar-free cook-
   and-serve or instant vanilla pudding mix

6 Phyllo Tart Shells (page 61)

1 cup diced fresh peaches or nectarines

½ cup fresh raspberries

½ cup Really Raspberry Sauce (page 55)

2 tablespoons sliced almonds

1. Use the milk to prepare the pudding according to package directions. Chill thoroughly before assembling the desserts.

2. Spoon a scant ⅓ cup of the pudding into each tart shell. Combine the peaches and raspberries and spoon ¼ cup of the mixture over the pudding in each shell. Drizzle some of the sauce over each tart and top with a sprinkling of almonds. Serve immediately.

Nutritional Facts (per serving)
Calories: 140   *Carbohydrates:* 25g   *Cholesterol:* 2mg   *Fat:* 2.4g   *Sat Fat:* 0.4g
Fiber: 2.4g   *Protein:* 4.6g   *Sodium:* 384mg   *Calcium:* 101mg
    Diabetic exchanges: 1½ carbohydrate, ½ fat

Chocolate Pudding Tarts

1¾ cups nonfat or low-fat milk

1 package (4-serving size) sugar-free instant or cook-and-serve chocolate pudding mix

6 Phyllo Tart Shells (page 61)*

1½ cups fresh raspberries or sliced strawberries

¾ cup nonfat or light whipped topping

¼ cup light (reduced-sugar) chocolate syrup

2 tablespoons sliced almonds or chopped walnuts

1. Use the milk to prepare the pudding according to package directions. Chill thoroughly before assembling the desserts.

2. Spoon a scant ⅓ cup of the pudding into each tart shell. Spoon ¼ cup of the fruit over the pudding in each shell. Top each serving with a dollop of whipped topping, a drizzle of chocolate syrup, and a sprinkling of nuts. Serve immediately.

Nutritional Facts (per serving)

Calories: 164 *Carbohydrates:* 30g *Cholesterol:* 2mg *Fat:* 2.8g *Sat Fat:* 0.4g

Fiber: 2.8g *Protein:* 5g *Sodium:* 181mg *Calcium:* 102mg

Diabetic exchanges: 2 carbohydrate, ½ fat

*When making the shells, substitute ⅛ teaspoon ground cinnamon for the lemon rind.

Flaky Apple Pastries

YIELD: 40 PASTRIES

20-ounce can no-added-sugar or light
(reduced-sugar) apple pie filling,
chopped

½ cup raisins, dried sweetened cranberries,
or dried pitted sweet cherries

20 sheets (14 by 18 inches) phyllo pastry
(about 1 pound)

Butter-flavored cooking spray

1½ tablespoons sugar

½ teaspoon ground cinnamon

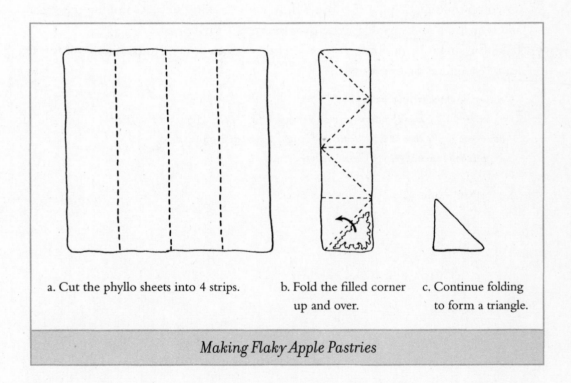

a. Cut the phyllo sheets into 4 strips.

b. Fold the filled corner up and over.

c. Continue folding to form a triangle.

Making Flaky Apple Pastries

NOTE: These pastries can be prepared ahead of time to the point of baking and then frozen until ready to bake. Let the pastries sit at room temperature for 15 minutes before placing in the oven.

1. Preheat the oven to 375 degrees.
2. Combine the pie filling and raisins and stir to mix. Set aside.
3. Spread the phyllo out on a clean dry surface. Cut the dough lengthwise into 4 long strips, about 3½ by 18 inches each. Cover the dough with a damp towel to prevent it from drying out as you work. (Remove strips as you need them, being sure to re-cover the remaining dough.)
4. Remove 2 strips of phyllo and stack one on top of the other. Spray the top strip with cooking spray. Spread 1 level tablespoon of the filling over the bottom right hand corner. Fold the filled corner up and over to the left. Continue folding in this manner until you form a triangle of dough. Repeat with the remaining filling and dough.
5. Coat a large baking sheet with cooking spray and arrange the pastries seam side down on the sheet. Spray the tops lightly with cooking spray. Combine the sugar and cinnamon and sprinkle some over the top of each pastry.
6. Bake for about 15 minutes, or until lightly browned. Let the pastries cool for at least 15 minutes before serving.

Nutritional Facts (per pastry)

Calories: 49   *Carbohydrates:* 9g   *Cholesterol:* 0mg   *Fat:* 1.1g   *Sat Fat:* 0.2g
Fiber: 0.5g   *Protein:* 0.9g   *Sodium:* 57mg   *Calcium:* 2mg
   Diabetic exchanges: ½ carbohydrate

4. Creamy Puddings, Mousses, and Trifles

Rich, creamy, and inviting, puddings are among the most popular of comfort foods. And from hearty noodle puddings to creamy custards and elegant mousses and trifles, many spins on the humble pudding are available to choose from. Made properly, puddings are among the most healthful of desserts, providing respectable amounts of protein and calcium. In addition, puddings are some of the easiest of desserts to trim down with regard to both sugar and fat. The recipes in this chapter combine sugar substitutes with low to moderate amounts of sugar to deliver optimal sweetness, flavor, and texture with a lot less carbohydrate. Fat is also kept to a minimum by using lower-fat versions of milk, yogurt, sour cream, cream cheese, and other dairy products. The result? A tempting selection of smooth and creamy desserts that are sure to become family favorites. But the proof is in the pudding. So whip up a creamy dish of comfort and enjoy a treat that is so satisfyingly sweet, you will find it hard to believe that it's also guilt-free!

Creamy Baked Custard

YIELD: 6 SERVINGS

2 cups nonfat or low-fat milk

½ cup sugar

Sugar substitute equal to ¼ cup sugar

1 cup evaporated nonfat or low-fat milk

1 cup fat-free egg substitute

1½ teaspoons vanilla extract

Ground nutmeg

1. Preheat the oven to 350 degrees.
2. Place the milk, sugar, and sugar substitute in a large bowl and whisk to dissolve the sugar. Whisk in the remaining ingredients, except the nutmeg.
3. Coat a 1½-quart casserole dish with cooking spray and pour the mixture into the dish. Sprinkle some nutmeg over the top. Place the casserole dish in a large pan filled with 1 inch of hot water.
4. Bake for about 1 hour, or until a sharp knife inserted midway between the rim and center of the dish comes out clean. Let the custard cool at room temperature for 30 minutes. Then cover and chill for several hours before serving.

Nutritional Facts (per ⅔-cup serving)
Calories: 146 *Carbohydrates:* 26g *Cholesterol:* 3mg *Fat:* 0.2g *Sat Fat:* 0.1g
Fiber: 0g *Protein:* 10g *Sodium:* 175mg *Calcium:* 237mg
Diabetic exchanges: 2 carbohydrate

Apple-Pecan Bread Pudding

4 cups stale oat bran or oatmeal bread cubes

1 cup chopped peeled apple

½ cup chopped toasted pecans (page 25)

⅓ cup sugar

Sugar substitute equal to ⅓ cup sugar

2 cups nonfat or low-fat milk

¾ cup fat-free egg substitute

1 teaspoon vanilla extract

TOPPING

1 tablespoon sugar

½ teaspoon ground cinnamon

1. Preheat the oven to 350 degrees.
2. Place the bread cubes, apple, and pecans in a large bowl and toss to mix. Place the sugar, sugar substitute, milk, egg substitute, and vanilla in a medium bowl and whisk to mix well. Pour the milk mixture over the bread mixture and stir gently to mix. Set aside for 10 minutes.
3. Coat an 8-by-8-inch (2-quart) dish with cooking spray and pour the bread mixture into the dish. Combine the topping ingredients and sprinkle over the pudding.
4. Place the dish in a large pan filled with 1 inch of hot water. Bake uncovered for about 50 minutes, or until a sharp knife inserted in the center of the dish comes out clean. Let the pudding sit at room temperature for at least 40 minutes before cutting into squares and serving. Serve warm or chilled.

Nutritional Facts (per serving)
Calories: 155   *Carbohydrates:* 22g   *Cholesterol:* 1mg   *Fat:* 5.4g   *Sat Fat:* 0.6g
Fiber: 1.5g   *Protein:* 6g   *Sodium:* 162mg   *Calcium:* 90mg
   Diabetic exchanges: 1½ carbohydrate, 1 fat

Chocolate Bread Pudding

4 cups stale oat bran or oatmeal bread cubes

½ cup chopped toasted pecans (page 25) or
    ¼ cup pecans plus ¼ cup chocolate chips

⅓ cup brown sugar

Sugar substitute equal to ½ cup sugar

¼ cup Dutch-processed cocoa powder

½ teaspoon ground cinnamon

2⅓ cups nonfat or low-fat milk

¾ cup fat-free egg substitute

1½ teaspoons vanilla extract

1 tablespoon sugar

1. Preheat the oven to 350 degrees.
2. Place the bread cubes and pecans in a large bowl and toss to mix. Place the sugar, sugar substitute, cocoa, and cinnamon in a medium bowl. Add half of the milk and whisk to mix well. Add the remaining milk, egg substitute, and vanilla and whisk again. Pour the milk mixture over the bread mixture and stir gently to mix. Set aside for 10 minutes.
3. Coat an 8-by-8-inch (2-quart) dish with cooking spray and pour the bread mixture into the dish. Sprinkle the sugar over the pudding.
4. Place the dish in a large pan filled with 1 inch of hot water. Bake uncovered for about 45 to 50 minutes, or until a sharp knife inserted in the center of the dish comes out clean. Let the pudding sit at room temperature for at least 40 minutes before cutting into squares and serving. Serve warm or chilled. Top each serving with some light whipped topping if desired.

Nutritional Facts (per serving)

Calories: 159   Carbohydrates: 22g   Cholesterol: 1mg   Fat: 5.7g   Sat Fat: 0.7g
Fiber: 2g   Protein: 6.8g   Sodium: 141mg   Calcium: 109mg
   Diabetic exchanges: 1½ carbohydrate, 1 fat

Baked Pumpkin Custard

1 cup canned or cooked mashed pumpkin

½ cup light brown sugar

Sugar substitute equal to ¼ cup sugar

1 teaspoon pumpkin pie spice

12-ounce can evaporated nonfat or
   low-fat milk

½ cup nonfat or low-fat milk

1 cup fat-free egg substitute

1½ teaspoons vanilla extract

TOPPINGS (OPTIONAL)

½ cup Honey-Orange Sauce (page 88)

¼ cup chopped toasted pecans (page 25)

1. Preheat the oven to 350 degrees.
2. Place the pumpkin, brown sugar, sugar substitute, and pie spice in a large bowl and stir with a wire whisk until smooth. Whisk in the remaining ingredients.
3. Coat a 1½-quart casserole dish with cooking spray and pour the pumpkin mixture into the dish. Place the dish in a large pan filled with 1 inch of hot water. Bake uncovered for about 1 hour, or until a sharp knife inserted near the center of the custard comes out clean. Let the custard cool to room temperature and then cover and chill for several hours before serving. If desired, top each serving with some of the warm sauce and pecans just before serving.

Nutritional Facts (per ⅔-cup serving)

Calories: 155 *Carbohydrates:* 29g *Cholesterol:* 2mg *Fat:* 0.3g *Sat Fat:* 0.2g

Fiber: 1.2g *Protein:* 9.5g *Sodium:* 169mg *Calcium:* 233mg

    Diabetic exchanges: 2 carbohydrate

Polenta Pudding

YIELD: 8 SERVINGS

¼ cup plus 2 tablespoons yellow cornmeal

2½ cups nonfat or low-fat milk

1 cup evaporated nonfat or low-fat milk

¼ cup plus 2 tablespoons honey

1 cup fat-free egg substitute

Sugar substitute equal to ¼ cup sugar

1½ teaspoons vanilla extract

⅓ cup golden raisins

Ground nutmeg

1. Preheat the oven to 350 degrees.
2. Place the cornmeal in a 2½-quart nonstick pot and slowly stir in the milk and evaporated milk. Cook over medium heat, stirring constantly, for 10 to 12 minutes or until the mixture comes to a boil. Reduce the heat to low and continue cooking and stirring for a couple of minutes more, or until slightly thickened. Slowly stir in the honey.
3. Place the egg substitute in a medium bowl and whisk in 1 cup of the hot cornmeal mixture. Slowly whisk the egg mixture back into the pudding. Cook and stir for a couple of minutes, or until slightly thickened. Remove the pot from the heat and stir in the sugar substitute, vanilla, and raisins.
4. Coat a 2-quart casserole dish with cooking spray and pour the pudding into the dish. Sprinkle some nutmeg over the top. Place the dish in a pan filled with 1 inch of hot water.
5. Bake uncovered for 1 hour, or until a sharp knife inserted near the center of the dish comes out clean. Allow the pudding to sit at room temperature for at least 45 minutes. Serve warm or refrigerate for several hours and serve chilled. Refrigerate any leftovers.

Nutritional Facts (per ⅔-cup serving)
Calories: 153   *Carbohydrates:* 30g   *Cholesterol:* 3mg   *Fat:* 0.4g   *Sat Fat:* 0.2g
Fiber: 0.7g   *Protein:* 9g   *Sodium:* 142mg   *Calcium:* 201mg
   Diabetic exchanges: 2 carbohydrate

Cherry-Cheese Kugel

For variety, substitute a 15-ounce can of peaches or apricots, drained and diced, for the cherries.

YIELD: 9 SERVINGS

4 ounces medium or wide no-yolk
    egg noodles

8-ounce block nonfat or reduced-fat
    (Neufchâtel) cream cheese, warmed to
    room temperature

⅓ cup sugar

Sugar substitute equal to ¼ cup sugar

1 cup nonfat or low-fat cottage cheese

1 cup fat-free egg substitute

1 teaspoon vanilla extract

1½ cups fresh or frozen (unthawed) pitted
    sweet cherries, halved

TOPPING

1 tablespoon sugar

2 tablespoons finely ground almonds
    or pecans

Butter-flavored cooking spray

1. Preheat the oven to 350 degrees.
2. Cook the noodles until tender according to package directions. Drain, rinse with cool water, and drain again. Set aside.
3. Place the cream cheese, sugar, and sugar substitute in a large bowl and beat with an electric mixer until smooth. Beat in the cottage cheese, egg substitute, and vanilla extract. Stir in the noodles and then the cherries.
4. Coat an 8-by-8-inch (2-quart) casserole dish with cooking spray and spread the noodle mixture in the dish. Combine the sugar and almonds or pecans and sprinkle over the top. Spray the top lightly with cooking spray.
5. Cover the dish loosely with aluminum foil and bake for 30 minutes. Remove the foil and bake for an additional 15 minutes, or until bubbly around the edges and lightly browned on top. Let cool for at least 40 minutes before cutting into squares and serving. Serve warm or at room temperature, refrigerating any leftovers.

Nutritional Facts (per serving)

Calories: 163   *Carbohydrates:* 25g   *Cholesterol:* 4mg   *Fat:* 1.2g   *Sat Fat:* 0.1g

Fiber: 1.2g   *Protein:* 9g   *Sodium:* 261mg   *Calcium:* 111mg

    Diabetic exchanges: 1½ carbohydrate

Raisin-Rice Pudding

3 cups nonfat or low-fat milk

½ cup basmati or Arborio white rice

Pinch salt

⅓ cup dark raisins

Sugar substitute equal to ½ cup sugar

¼ cup plus 2 tablespoons fat-free egg substitute

¾ teaspoon vanilla extract

Ground nutmeg (optional)

1. Place the milk, rice, and salt in a 2½-quart nonstick pot and place over medium heat. Cover and cook, stirring frequently, until the milk just begins to bubble around the edges. Reduce the heat to low and simmer covered for 25 minutes, or until the rice is tender. Add the raisins and simmer for 3 minutes more.

2. Place about ⅓ cup of the rice mixture in a small dish and stir in the sugar substitute, egg substitute, and vanilla. Add the mixture back to the pot and cook, stirring constantly, for a couple of minutes until the mixture thickens.

3. Allow the pudding to cool for 20 minutes and then stir in a little more milk if the mixture seems too thick. Serve warm or chilled, topping each serving with a sprinkling of nutmeg if desired.

Nutritional Facts (per ⅔-cup serving)
Calories: 136   Carbohydrates: 26g   Cholesterol: 2mg   Fat: 0.4g   Sat Fat: 0.2g
Fiber: 0.5g   Protein: 7.2g   Sodium: 120mg   Calcium: 164mg
   Diabetic exchanges: 2 carbohydrate

Phyllo Custard Cups

2 ¼ cups nonfat or low-fat milk

¼ cup plus 1 tablespoon quick-cooking
  Cream of Wheat or farina cereal

½ cup plus 1 tablespoon fat-free egg
  substitute

Sugar substitute equal to ½ cup sugar

3 tablespoons finely chopped dried apricots

⅛ teaspoon ground nutmeg

Pinch salt

6 Phyllo Tart Shells (page 61)

½ cup Honey-Orange Sauce (page 88)

1. Place the milk in a 2-quart pot and cook over medium heat, stirring frequently, until the milk begins to boil. Whisk in the cereal, reduce the heat to low, and cook, stirring constantly, for several minutes, or until the mixture thickens slightly.

2. Place the egg substitute in a small bowl and stir in ½ cup of the hot milk mixture. Return the egg mixture to the pot and cook, stirring constantly, for a couple of minutes, or until the mixture thickens slightly.

3. Remove the pot from the heat and stir in the sugar substitute, apricots, nutmeg, and salt. Let the custard cool at room temperature for 15 minutes.

4. To assemble the desserts, stir the custard and spoon a scant half cup of the mixture into each tart shell. Drizzle 1½ tablespoons of the hot syrup over the custard and the edges of the pastry. Serve immediately.

Nutritional Facts (per serving)
Calories: 176 *Carbohydrates:* 31g *Cholesterol:* 2mg *Fat:* 1.5g *Sat Fat:* 0.3g
Fiber: 1g *Protein:* 8g *Sodium:* 177mg *Calcium:* 140mg
Diabetic exchanges: 2 carbohydrate

NOTE: This dessert should be assembled just before serving. The custard and syrup can be made in advance and reheated in a microwave oven at the last minute. The shells can be made several days before and stored in an airtight container.

Honey-Orange Sauce

YIELD: 1¼ CUPS

1 tablespoon cornstarch

1 cup orange juice

¼ cup honey

Sugar substitute equal to ¼ cup sugar

1. Place the cornstarch in a small pot, add a tablespoon of the juice, and stir to dissolve the cornstarch. Stir in the remaining juice, honey, and sugar substitute.
2. Place over medium heat and cook, stirring frequently, for several minutes or until the sauce is thickened and bubbly. Serve warm.

Nutritional Facts (per tablespoon)
Calories: 21   *Carbohydrates:* 5g   *Cholesterol:* 0mg   *Fat:* 0g   *Sat Fat:* 0g   *Fiber:* 0g
Protein: 0.1g   *Sodium:* 0mg   *Calcium:* 2mg
Diabetic exchanges: ⅓ carbohydrate

Light Tapioca Pudding

YIELD: 5 SERVINGS

3 tablespoons quick-cooking tapioca

⅓ cup nonfat dry milk powder

¼ cup sugar

Sugar substitute equal to ¼ cup sugar

3 cups nonfat or low-fat milk

¼ cup plus 2 tablespoons fat-free egg substitute

1 teaspoon vanilla extract

Ground nutmeg (optional)

1. Place all of the ingredients except for the vanilla and nutmeg in a 2½-quart microwave-safe bowl and stir to mix. Set aside for 5 minutes.
2. Place the bowl in a microwave oven and cook at high power for 8 to 10 minutes,

stirring every 2 minutes, until the mixture comes to a *full* boil. Stir in the vanilla and let the pudding sit for 20 minutes without stirring.

3. Stir the pudding and transfer to a covered container. Chill for several hours, or until thick and creamy. (The pudding will thicken more as it cools.) If desired, top each serving with a sprinkling of nutmeg just before serving.

Nutritional Facts (per ⅔-cup serving)
Calories: 138   *Carbohydrates:* 25g   *Cholesterol:* 4mg   *Fat:* 0.3g   *Sat Fat:* 0.2g
Fiber: 0g   *Protein:* 8.4g   *Sodium:* 138mg   *Calcium:* 242 mg
   Diabetic exchanges: 1½ carbohydrate

Tapioca Pudding Parfaits

YIELD: 6 SERVINGS

1 recipe Light Tapioca Pudding (page 88)
1½ cups no-sugar-added or light (reduced-sugar) cherry pie filling
   or coarsely chopped light apple pie filling

1. Place ¼ cup of the pudding in each of six 8-ounce wine glasses. Top the pudding in each glass with 2 tablespoons of the pie filling. Divide the remaining pudding between the glasses and top with the remaining pie filling.

2. Cover and chill for at least 1 hour before serving.

Nutritional Facts (per ¾-cup serving)
Calories: 135   *Carbohydrates:* 25g   *Cholesterol:* 3mg   *Fat:* 0.4g   *Sat Fat:* 0.2g
Fiber: 0.4g   *Protein:* 7g   *Sodium:* 150mg   *Calcium:* 202mg
   Diabetic exchanges: 1½ carbohydrate

Peanut-Butter Mousse

1¼ cups nonfat or low-fat milk

½ cup nonfat or light sour cream

1 package (4-serving size) sugar-free instant white chocolate pudding mix

4 ounces reduced-fat (Neufchâtel) cream cheese

½ to ⅔ cup peanut butter

Sugar substitute equal to 3 tablespoons sugar

3 cups nonfat or light whipped topping

¼ cup shaved or finely chopped dark chocolate or ½ cup crumbled chocolate graham crackers or chocolate wafer cookies

1. Place the milk, sour cream, and pudding mix in a large bowl and beat at low speed with an electric mixer for 1 minute. Add the cream cheese and beat for an additional minute. Beat in the peanut butter and sugar substitute. Add half of the whipped topping and beat just until it is mixed in. Fold in the remaining whipped topping.

2. Divide the mixture between eight 8-ounce wine glasses. Cover and chill for at least 1 hour. Top each serving with a sprinkling of the shaved chocolate or cookie crumbs just before serving.

Nutritional Facts (per ⅔-cup serving)
Calories: 242   *Carbohydrates:* 24g   *Cholesterol:* 11mg   *Fat:* 13g   *Sat Fat:* 4g
Fiber: 1.4g   *Protein:* 8g   *Sodium:* 275mg   *Calcium:* 93mg
Diabetic exchanges: 1½ carbohydrate, 2½ fat

Spiced Pumpkin Mousse

YIELD: 5 SERVINGS

1 package (4-serving size) instant sugar-free butterscotch pudding mix

1 cup cooked mashed or canned pumpkin

1 cup nonfat or low-fat milk

1 to 1½ teaspoons pumpkin pie spice

2 cups nonfat or light whipped topping

5 gingersnap cookies

1. Place the pudding mix, pumpkin, milk, and pie spice in a large bowl. Stir with a wire whisk for 2 minutes. Place the mixture in the refrigerator for 5 to 10 minutes to thicken.

2. Fold the whipped topping into the pumpkin mixture. Divide the mixture among five 8-ounce wine glasses and chill for at least 2 hours before serving. Crumble a gingersnap cookie over the top of each dessert just before serving.

Nutritional Facts (per ⅔-cup serving)

Calories: 132 Carbohydrates: 27g Cholesterol: 1mg Fat: 1.8g Sat Fat: 3g
Fiber: 1.4g Protein: 2.5g Sodium: 371mg Calcium: 73mg
  Diabetic exchanges: 2 carbohydrate

Ambrosia Delite

YIELD: 6 SERVINGS

11-ounce can mandarin oranges

8-ounce can crushed pineapple

1 package (4-serving size) sugar-free orange gelatin

¾ cup light coconut cream, pineapple, or vanilla yogurt

⅓ cup chopped toasted pecans (page 25)

2 cups nonfat or light whipped topping

1. Drain the oranges and pineapples well, reserving the juice. Bring the juice to a boil and pour into a large bowl. Sprinkle the gelatin over the top and whisk for 2 min-

utes, or until the gelatin is completely dissolved. Set aside for 15 minutes to cool to room temperature.

2. Whisk the yogurt into the gelatin and then chill for about 30 minutes, or until the mixture is the consistency of pudding. Whisk the gelatin mixture until smooth and then fold in the drained oranges and pineapple along with the pecans. Fold in the whipped topping.

3. Divide the mixture between six 8-ounce wine glasses. Cover and chill for at least 3 hours before serving.

Nutritional Facts (per serving)
Calories: 150   *Carbohydrates:* 23g   *Cholesterol:* 1mg   *Fat:* 5.5g   *Sat Fat:* 0.4g
Fiber: 1.3g   *Protein:* 3.4g   *Sodium:* 75mg   *Calcium:* 65mg
   Diabetic exchanges: 1½ carbohydrate, 1 fat

Really Raspberry Parfaits

YIELD: 4 SERVINGS

1 cup light raspberry yogurt

½ cup nonfat or light whipped topping

2 cups fresh raspberries, rinsed and patted dry

2 tablespoons sliced almonds

1. Place the yogurt in a bowl and fold in the whipped topping.

2. Place ¼ cup of raspberries in each of four 8-ounce wine glasses. Top the berries in each glass with 3 tablespoons of the yogurt mixture. Repeat the layers and top each serving with a sprinkling of almonds. Serve immediately.

Nutritional Facts (per serving)
Calories: 83   *Carbohydrates:* 14g   *Cholesterol:* 1mg   *Fat:* 2.3g   *Sat Fat:* 0.1g
Fiber: 4.5g   *Protein:* 2.7g   *Sodium:* 29mg   *Calcium:* 83mg
   Diabetic exchanges: 1 carbohydrate, ½ fat

Blueberry Bavarian

3½ cups fresh or frozen (unthawed)
   blueberries

1 tablespoon sugar

2 tablespoons orange juice

Sugar substitute equal to ⅓ cup sugar

1 cup light sour cream

3 cups nonfat or light whipped topping

1. Place the berries, sugar, and orange juice in a 2-quart nonstick pot and stir to mix well. Place over medium heat, cover, and cook, stirring occasionally for about 5 minutes, or until the berries have softened and released their juices.

2. Increase the heat to medium-high and cook uncovered, mashing the berries with the back of a spoon and stirring frequently for several minutes, or until the mixture is reduced by about one-fourth. Lower the heat to medium, and cook, stirring frequently for several minutes more, or until the mixture has a puddinglike consistency and is reduced to about 1¼ cups.

3. Transfer the berry mixture to a covered container and refrigerate for several hours, or until well chilled. When ready to assemble the desserts, fold the sugar substitute and sour cream into the berry mixture and then fold in the whipped topping. Divide the dessert between six 8-ounce wine glasses. Cover and refrigerate for at least 1 hour before serving.

Nutritional Facts (per ¾-cup serving)
Calories: 163   *Carbohydrates:* 29g   *Cholesterol:* 6mg   *Fat:* 2.6g   *Sat Fat:* 1.4g
Fiber: 2.4g   *Protein:* 1.8g   *Sodium:* 47mg   *Calcium:* 16mg
   Diabetic exchanges: 2 carbohydrate, ½ fat

Mocha Mousse

1 cup nonfat or low-fat milk

½ cup nonfat or light sour cream

1 package (4-serving size) sugar-free instant chocolate pudding mix

⅛ teaspoon ground cinnamon

4 ounces block-style nonfat or reduced-fat (Neufchâtel) cream cheese, softened to room temperature

3 to 4 tablespoons coffee liqueur

3 cups nonfat or light whipped topping

½ cup crumbled chocolate graham cracker or wafer cookies or 3 tablespoons shaved dark chocolate (optional)

1. Place the milk, sour cream, pudding mix, and cinnamon in a large bowl. Beat with an electric mixer for about 1 minute. Add the cream cheese, beat until smooth, and then beat in the liqueur.

2. Add half of the whipped topping and beat at low speed for several seconds, or just until the topping is mixed in. Gently fold in the rest of the whipped topping.

3. Divide the mousse between six 8-ounce wine glasses. Cover and chill for at least 1 hour before serving. If desired, top each dessert with some of the cookie crumbs or shaved chocolate just before serving.

Nutritional Facts (per serving)

Calories: 165   *Carbohydrates:* 27g   *Cholesterol:* 2mg   *Fat:* 1.3g   *Sat Fat:* 0.5g

Fiber: 0.2g   *Protein:* 5g   *Sodium:* 202mg   *Calcium:* 134mg

Diabetic exchanges: 2 carbohydrate

Black Forest Mousse

YIELD: 6 SERVINGS

1 package (4-serving size) sugar-free instant chocolate pudding mix

1½ cups nonfat or low-fat milk

1½ cups no-sugar-added or light (reduced-sugar) cherry pie filling

2¼ cups nonfat or light whipped topping

2 tablespoons shaved or finely chopped dark chocolate

1. Place the pudding and milk in a large bowl and whisk for 2 minutes to mix well. Place the pudding in the refrigerator for at least 10 minutes to thicken. Fold the cherry pie filling into the pudding and then fold in 1½ cups of the whipped topping.
2. Divide the mixture between six 8-ounce wine glasses and top each serving with some of the remaining whipped topping and a sprinkling of chocolate. Cover and chill for at least 1 hour before serving.

Nutritional Facts (per ¾-cup serving)
Calories: 130   *Carbohydrates:* 24g   *Cholesterol:* 1mg   *Fat:* 2.1g   *Sat Fat:* 0.7g
Fiber: 1g   *Protein:* 2.4g   *Sodium:* 107mg   *Calcium:* 76mg
   Diabetic exchanges: 1½ carbohydrate

Triple Berry Mousse

YIELD: 6 SERVINGS

1¾ cups frozen strawberries, coarsely
   chopped, thawed

¾ cup frozen raspberries, thawed

½ cup reduced-calorie cranberry juice
   cocktail

1 envelope (¼ ounce) unflavored gelatin

4 ounces nonfat or reduced-fat (Neufchâtel)
   cream cheese

½ cup nonfat or light sour cream

Sugar substitute equal to ½ cup plus
   2 tablespoons sugar

2 cups nonfat or light whipped topping

1. Drain the juices from the strawberries and raspberries and mix with the cranberry juice. Place 2 tablespoons of the juice mixture in a blender and sprinkle the gelatin over the top. Set aside for 2 minutes.

2. Bring the remaining juice to a boil and pour over the blender mixture. Blend for 1 minute, or until the gelatin is completely dissolved. Set aside for 10 minutes to cool slightly.

3. Add the cream cheese, sour cream, and sugar substitute to the blender mixture and blend until smooth. Transfer the mixture to a large bowl. Mash the berries and add to the gelatin mixture. Place in the refrigerator for about 40 minutes, or until the mixture is the consistency of pudding. Whisk well and then fold in the whipped topping.

4. Divide the mousse between six 8-ounce wine glasses and chill for at least 2 hours before serving.

Nutritional Facts (per ⅔-cup serving)
Calories: 115   *Carbohydrates:* 21g   *Cholesterol:* 1mg   *Fat:* 1g   *Sat Fat:* 0.2g
Fiber: 1.8g   *Protein:* 5.3g   *Sodium:* 123mg   *Calcium:* 91mg
   Diabetic exchanges: 1½ carbohydrate

Banana Pudding Parfaits

2 cups nonfat or low-fat milk

1 package (4-serving size) sugar-free cook-
   and-serve or instant vanilla pudding mix

1 cup sliced bananas

12 low-fat vanilla wafers, crumbled

½ cup nonfat or light whipped topping
   (optional)

1. Use the milk to prepare the pudding according to package directions and then refrigerate until well chilled.
2. To assemble the parfaits, place 2 tablespoons of the pudding in the bottom of each
   of four 8-ounce wine glasses.
3. Top the pudding in each glass with 2 tablespoons of banana slices, 1½ crumbled
   vanilla wafers and 3 tablespoons of pudding. Repeat the banana, vanilla wafer, and
   pudding layers. Serve immediately or cover and chill for up to 3 hours before serving, topping each dessert with some of the whipped topping if desired.

Nutritional Facts (per serving)
Calories: 142 *Carbohydrates:* 28g *Cholesterol:* 2mg *Fat:* 1.7g *Sat Fat:* 0.2g
Fiber: 1g *Protein:* 5.3g *Sodium:* 225mg *Calcium:* 157mg
  Diabetic exchanges: 2 carbohydrate

Strawberry Tiramisu

PUDDING MIXTURE

2 cups nonfat or low-fat milk

1 package (4-serving size) sugar-free instant
   vanilla pudding mix

4 ounces reduced-fat (Neufchâtel)
   cream cheese, brought to room
   temperature

BERRY MIXTURE
2¼ cups frozen strawberries, coarsely
  chopped and thawed
Sugar substitute equal to 2 tablespoons
  sugar

9 ladyfingers (about 2¼ ounces)
¼ cup plus 2 tablespoons coffee liqueur
1 cup plus 2 tablespoons nonfat or light
  whipped topping
¾ teaspoon cocoa powder

1. Place the milk and pudding mix in a medium bowl and beat at low speed with an electric mixer for 2 minutes. Beat in the cream cheese and set aside.

2. Combine the strawberries and their juices and the sugar substitute in a small bowl and mash slightly. Set aside.

3. To assemble the desserts, place 1½ tablespoons of the strawberry mixture in the bottom of each of six 8-ounce wine glasses. Crumble ¾ of a ladyfinger over the berries in each glass. Drizzle 1½ teaspoons of the liqueur over the ladyfinger layer and then cover with 3 tablespoons of the pudding mixture. Repeat the berry, ladyfinger, liqueur, and pudding layers.

4. Spread 3 tablespoons of the whipped topping over the top of each dessert and sift some of the cocoa over the top. Cover and chill for at least 1½ hours before serving.

Nutritional Facts (per serving)
Calories: 227   *Carbohydrates:* 32g   *Cholesterol:* 35mg   *Fat:* 5.8g   *Sat Fat:* 3.1g
Fiber: 1.6g   *Protein:* 6g   *Sodium:* 396mg   *Calcium:* 136mg
  Diabetic exchanges: 2 carbohydrate, 1 fat

Pineapple Fluff

YIELD: 9 SERVINGS

2 cans (8 ounces each) crushed pineapple
  in juice
1 package (4-serving size) sugar-free lemon
  gelatin

¾ cup nonfat or light sour cream
⅓ cup chopped toasted pecans (page 25)
2 cups nonfat or light whipped topping

1. Drain the pineapple well, reserving the juice. Place the juice in a small pot and bring to a boil.

2. Place the gelatin mix in a medium heatproof bowl and add the boiling juice. Stir the mixture with a wire whisk for at least 1 minute, or until the gelatin is completely dissolved. Set the mixture aside for 20 minutes, or until it reaches room temperature.

3. Stir the drained pineapple, sour cream, and pecans into the gelatin mixture and refrigerate for 45 minutes, or until it is the consistency of pudding. Stir well, and then fold in the whipped topping. Pour the mixture into an 8-by-8-inch (2-quart) glass dish and chill for several hours, or until firm. Cut into squares to serve.

Nutritional Facts (per serving)

Calories: 111   *Carbohydrates:* 17g   *Cholesterol:* 0mg   *Fat:* 3.2g   *Sat Fat:* 0.3g

Fiber: 1g   *Protein:* 2.5g   *Sodium:* 48mg   *Calcium:* 34mg

Diabetic exchanges: 1 carbohydrate, ½ fat

Banana-Pineapple Pudding

YIELD: 9 SERVINGS

1 package (4-serving size) sugar-free instant vanilla pudding mix

1½ cups nonfat or low-fat milk

1 cup nonfat or light ricotta cheese

24 low-fat vanilla wafers

2 medium bananas, sliced

8-ounce can crushed pineapple in juice, drained

⅓ cup light vanilla yogurt

2 cups nonfat or light whipped topping

3 tablespoons sliced almonds (optional)

1. Place the pudding mix, milk, and ricotta cheese in a medium bowl and beat at low speed with an electric mixer for 2 minutes. Set aside.

2. Arrange the vanilla wafers in a single layer over the bottom and up the sides of an 8-by-8-inch (2-quart) casserole dish. Spread the pudding over the vanilla wafers and top with first the bananas and then the pineapple.

3. To make the topping fold the yogurt into the whipped topping and spread the mixture over the top of the pudding. Sprinkle the almonds over the top. Cover and refrigerate for 2 to 5 hours before serving.

Nutritional Facts (per 1-cup serving)
Calories: 175   *Carbohydrates:* 29g   *Cholesterol:* 3mg   *Fat:* 3.4g   *Sat Fat:* 0.5g
Fiber: 1.4g   *Protein:* 7.5g   *Sodium:* 225mg   *Calcium:* 215mg
Diabetic exchanges: 2 carbohydrate, ½ fat

⁘ Apple-Apricot Pudding Torte ⁘

YIELD: 9 SERVINGS

8-ounce block reduced-fat (Neufchâtel) cheese, softened to room temperature

1¼ cups nonfat or low-fat milk

1 package (4-serving size) sugar-free instant vanilla pudding mix

¼ cup low-sugar apricot jam or fruit spread

3 tablespoons apricot brandy

18 ladyfingers (about 4½ ounces)

1¼ cups canned no-added-sugar or light (reduced-sugar) apple pie filling, finely chopped

2 cups nonfat or light whipped topping

3 tablespoons sliced toasted almonds or chopped toasted pecans (page 25)

1. Place the cream cheese in a medium-sized bowl and beat with an electric mixer until smooth. Still beating, gradually add the milk and beat until smooth. Add the pudding mix and beat for another minute, or until well mixed and thickened. Set aside.
2. Place the apricot jam and the brandy in a mini blender jar and blend until smooth. Set aside.
3. Split the ladyfingers open and arrange half of them, split side up, in a single layer over the bottom of an 8-inch square (2-quart) dish. Drizzle half of the apricot mixture over the ladyfingers and then spread with half of the pudding mixture. Repeat the ladyfinger, apricot, and pudding layers.

4. Spread the pie filling over the pudding layer, then spread the whipped topping over the dessert. Sprinkle the nuts over the top.

5. Cover the dish and refrigerate for at least 8 hours, or overnight, before cutting into squares and serving

Nutritional Facts (per serving)

Calories: 212   *Carbohydrates:* 28g   *Cholesterol:* 44mg   *Fat:* 8g   *Sat Fat:* 3.9g
Fiber: 0.9g   *Protein:* 5.3g   *Sodium:* 362mg   *Calcium:* 81mg
   Diabetic exchanges: 2 carbohydrate, 1½ fat

∴ Razzleberry Trifle ∴

YIELD: 12 SERVINGS

2½ cups sliced fresh strawberries

1 cup fresh or frozen (thawed) raspberries

Sugar substitute equal to 2 tablespoons sugar

3 cups nonfat or low-fat milk

1 package (6-serving size) cook-and-serve or instant vanilla pudding mix

10 slices (½ inch each) fat-free loaf cake or low-fat pound cake

¼ cup low-sugar raspberry jam

TOPPING

2 cups nonfat or light whipped topping

½ cup light vanilla yogurt

2 to 3 tablespoons sliced almonds

1. Place the berries and sugar substitute in a medium bowl and toss to mix. Set aside for 20 minutes to let the juices develop.

2. Use the milk to prepare the pudding according to package directions. If using cook-and-serve pudding, chill the pudding before proceeding with the recipe.

3. Spread one side of each cake slice with some of the jam. Arrange half of the cake slices, jam side up, over the bottom of a 3-quart trifle bowl or decorative glass bowl. Top the cake with half of the fruit and half of the pudding. Repeat the cake, fruit, and pudding layers.

4. To make the topping, place the whipped topping in a medium bowl and fold in the yogurt. Swirl the mixture over the top of the trifle. Cover and chill for at least 2 hours before serving.

Nutritional Facts (per ⅞-cup serving)
Calories: 151 *Carbohydrates:* 31g *Cholesterol:* 1mg *Fat:* 1.5g *Sat Fat:* 0.1g
Fiber: 2g *Protein:* 4.2g *Sodium:* 210mg *Calcium:* 122mg
Diabetic exchanges: 2 carbohydrate

5. Colossal Cookies

ookies are the perfect treat when you crave a bite of something sweet. Unfortunately, cookies are one the most difficult treats to lighten up with respect to both carbohydrate and fat, since these ingredients give cookies their structure and volume. So how can you make cookies more appropriate for a diabetic diet? This chapter will show you how. These recipes get a fiber boost from ingredients like oats and whole-wheat pastry flour, which replaces the nutrient-poor white flour used in traditional recipes. Emphasis is also placed on using "good" fats like canola oil and soft trans-free margarine instead of shortening. And wholesome additions like nuts and dried fruits add their own unique nutritional benefits. As for sugar, the recipes in this chapter do contain moderate amounts of sugar and other sweeteners like molasses or maple syrup, which is necessary for a good texture.

Even though these recipes contain some sugar, you will see that the cookies in this chapter compare favorably with the "sugar-free" cookies sold in most grocery stores with regard to total carbs and calories. Moreover, you will get a nutritionally superior cookie, due to the inclusion of wholesome whole-grain ingredients and healthful fats—not to mention that fresh baked flavor that only homemade cookies have.

∴ *Make-Ahead Chocolate-Chip Cookies* ∴

You can make this dough in advance and keep it in the freezer so it's ready when you are.

YIELD: 48 COOKIES

½ cup margarine or butter

¾ cup light brown sugar

⅓ cup fat-free egg substitute

1 teaspoon vanilla extract

¾ cup whole-wheat pastry flour

½ cup oat flour

½ teaspoon baking soda

¾ cup semisweet chocolate chips

1 cup chopped walnuts

1. Place the margarine or butter and sugar in a medium bowl and beat until smooth. Beat in the egg substitute and vanilla extract.

2. In a separate bowl, combine the flours and baking soda and stir to mix well. Add the flour mixture to the margarine mixture and beat to mix well. Beat in the chocolate chips and walnuts. Place the dough in the freezer for at least 2 hours, or until ready to bake.

3. Drop slightly rounded teaspoons of the frozen dough onto a nonstick baking sheet. Bake at 350 degrees for about 8 minutes, or until golden brown. Let the cookies cool on the pan for 1 minute then transfer to wire racks to cool completely. Store in an airtight container.

Nutritional Facts (per cookie)
Calories: 66   Carbohydrates: 7.5g   Cholesterol: 0mg   Fat: 3.9g   Sat Fat: 0.9g
Fiber: 0.7g   Protein: 1.3g   Sodium: 33mg   Calcium: 6mg
Diabetic exchanges: ½ carbohydrate, ¾ fat

Applesauce Oatmeal Cookies

YIELD: 60 COOKIES

¼ cup plus 2 tablespoons margarine or
   butter

1 cup light brown sugar

¼ cup fat-free egg substitute

2 tablespoons applesauce

1 teaspoon vanilla extract

1½ cups old-fashioned (5-minute) oats

¾ cup whole-wheat pastry flour

½ teaspoon baking soda

½ teaspoon ground cinnamon

1 cup chopped walnuts

¾ cup dark raisins or chopped dried fruit

1. Preheat the oven to 350 degrees.
2. Place the margarine or butter and brown sugar in a medium bowl and beat until smooth. Beat in the egg substitute, applesauce, and vanilla extract.
3. In a separate bowl, combine the oats, flour, baking soda, and cinnamon and stir to mix well. Add the flour mixture to the margarine mixture and beat to mix well. Beat in the walnuts and raisins.
4. Drop slightly rounded teaspoons of dough onto a nonstick baking sheet. Bake for about 8 to 10 minutes or until golden brown. Let the cookies cool on the pan for 1 minute then transfer to wire racks to cool completely. Store in an airtight container.

Nutritional Facts (per cookie)

Calories: 54   *Carbohydrates:* 8g   *Cholesterol:* 0mg   *Fat:* 2.2g   *Sat Fat:* 0.3g

Fiber: 0.7g   *Protein:* 1.2g   *Sodium:* 24mg   *Calcium:* 6mg

   Diabetic exchanges: ½ carbohydrate, ½ fat

Molasses Oatmeal Cookies

½ cup margarine or butter

⅔ cup light brown sugar

¼ cup molasses

¼ cup fat-free egg substitute

2 cups quick-cooking (1-minute) oats

¾ cup whole-wheat pastry flour

1 teaspoon dried lemon rind

½ teaspoon ground cinnamon or ginger

¾ teaspoon baking soda

1. Place the margarine and brown sugar in a medium bowl and beat until smooth. Beat in the molasses and egg substitute.
2. In a separate bowl, combine the oats, flour, lemon rind, cinnamon or ginger, and baking soda and stir to mix. Add the flour mixture to the margarine mixture and beat to mix well.
3. Place the dough in the freezer for about 20 minutes or until firm enough to handle. Roll the dough into 1-inch balls and place 1½ inches apart on a nonstick baking sheet. Flatten the cookies to ¼-inch thickness with the bottom of a glass. (Dip the bottom of the glass lightly in sugar or in finely ground walnuts or pecans between cookies to prevent sticking.)
4. Bake at 350 degrees for about 10 to 12 minutes, or until golden brown. Cool on the pan for a couple of minutes, then transfer to wire racks to cool completely. Store in an airtight container.

Nutritional Facts (per cookie)

Calories: 49   *Carbohydrates:* 8g   *Cholesterol:* 0mg   *Fat:* 1.7g   *Sat Fat:* 0.5g
Fiber: 0.6g   *Protein:* 1g   *Sodium:* 39mg   *Calcium:* 8mg
  Diabetic exchanges: ½ carbohydrate, ⅓ fat

Pumpkin-Pecan Cookies

YIELD: 48 COOKIES

¼ cup margarine or butter

1 cup light brown sugar

¼ cup cooked mashed or canned pumpkin

2 tablespoons fat-free egg substitute

1 teaspoon vanilla extract

1½ cups whole-wheat pastry flour or
    unbleached flour

1 cup oat bran

1 to 1½ teaspoons pumpkin pie spice

¾ teaspoon baking soda

48 pecan halves

1. Place the margarine or butter and the brown sugar in a medium bowl and beat until smooth. Add the pumpkin, egg substitute, and vanilla and beat to mix well.

2. In a separate bowl, combine the flour, oat bran, pie spice, and baking soda and stir to mix. Add the flour mixture to the margarine mixture and beat to mix well. Place the mixture in the freezer for about 20 minutes, or until firm enough to shape.

3. Shape the dough into 48 balls, each slightly less than 1 inch in diameter. Coat a baking sheet with cooking spray and arrange the balls on the sheet, spacing them 3 inches apart. Press a pecan half into the center of each cookie.

4. Bake at 325 degrees for about 12 minutes, or until the bottoms are golden brown. Transfer the cookies to a wire rack to cool. Store in an airtight container.

Nutritional Facts (per cookie)

Calories: 55   *Carbohydrates:* 9g   *Cholesterol:* 0mg   *Fat:* 2.3g   *Sat Fat:* 0.4g

Fiber: 1g   *Protein:* 1g   *Sodium:* 30mg   *Calcium:* 7mg

Diabetic exchanges: ½ carbohydrate, ½ fat

Colossal Cookies · 107

Whole-Wheat Ginger Snaps

YIELD: 48 COOKIES

½ cup margarine or butter

⅔ cup light brown sugar

¼ cup molasses

¼ cup fat-free egg substitute

1½ cups whole-wheat pastry flour

1 cup oat bran

1½ to 2 teaspoons ground ginger

1 teaspoon ground cinnamon

¾ teaspoon baking soda

1. Place the margarine and brown sugar in a medium bowl and beat until smooth. Beat in the molasses and egg substitute.
2. In a separate bowl, combine the flour, oat bran, ginger, cinnamon, and baking soda and stir to mix. Add the flour mixture to the margarine mixture and beat to mix well.
3. Place the dough in the freezer for about 20 minutes, or until firm enough to handle. Roll the dough into 1-inch balls and place 1½ inches apart on a nonstick baking sheet. Flatten the cookies to ¼-inch thickness with the bottom of a glass. (Dip the bottom of the glass lightly in sugar between cookies to prevent sticking.)
4. Bake at 350 degrees for about 10 to 12 minutes, or until golden brown. Cool on the pan for a couple of minutes, then transfer to wire racks to cool completely. Store in an airtight container.

Nutritional Facts (per cookie)

Calories: 51   *Carbohydrates:* 9g   *Cholesterol:* 0mg   *Fat:* 1.8g   *Sat Fat:* 0.5g   *Fiber:* 1g

Protein: 1g   *Sodium:* 41mg   *Calcium:* 7mg

  Diabetic exchanges: ½ carbohydrate, ⅓ fat

Fruit & Nut Drops

1 cup plus 2 tablespoons whole-wheat
   pastry flour

⅔ cup light brown sugar

1 teaspoon baking soda

¼ cup plus 2 tablespoons pure maple syrup

2 tablespoons fat-free egg substitute or 1 egg
   white, beaten

1½ tablespoons orange juice

1 teaspoon vanilla extract

2 cups bran flake cereal

¾ cup chopped dried apricots

¾ cup chopped dried plums, raisins, dried
   cherries, or dried sweetened cranberries

1½ cups chopped toasted pecans (page 25)
   or chopped walnuts

1. Preheat the oven to 300 degrees.

2. Place the flour and brown sugar in a medium bowl and stir to mix well. Use the back of a spoon to press out the lumps in the brown sugar. Add the baking soda and stir to mix well.

3. In a separate bowl, combine the maple syrup, egg substitute or egg white, orange juice, and vanilla and stir to mix well. Add the maple syrup mixture to the flour mixture and stir to mix well. Stir in the cereal, fruits, and nuts.

4. Coat a large baking sheet with nonstick cooking spray and place rounded teaspoons of the dough onto the sheet, spacing the cookies 1½ inches apart. Flatten each cookie slightly with the tip of a spoon.

5. Bake one sheet at a time for about 14 minutes, or until the bottoms are golden brown. Let the cookies cool on the pan for 2 minutes, then transfer to wire racks to cool completely. Store in an airtight container.

Nutritional Facts (per cookie)

Calories: 57 *Carbohydrates:* 9g *Cholesterol:* 0mg *Fat:* 2.2g *Sat Fat:* 0.2g

Fiber: 1.2g *Protein:* 0.9g *Sodium:* 33mg *Calcium:* 8mg

   Diabetic exchanges: ½ carbohydrate, ½ fat

Sugar-free Treats and Your Diabetic Diet

Fueled by rising interest in lower-carb diets, manufacturers now offer a plethora of "sugar-free" cookies, candies, ice cream, and other confections. But is sugar-free all it's cracked up to be? Not always.

People are often surprised to discover that some sugar-free products have just as many calories as the products they are meant to replace. (This is why many of these products bear labels that state "Not for Weight Control.") How can this be? For one thing, extra fat is frequently added to make up for the flavor and texture that is lost when sugar is removed. In addition, most sugar-free cookies and baked goods still contain a high proportion of white flour, which adds carbs and calories.

What gives sugar-free products their sweetness? Many products contain "sugar alcohols" such as maltitol, sorbitol, and hydrogenated starch hydrolysates. These carbohydrate-based sweeteners are incompletely absorbed, so they provide about half the calories of sugar and they have a milder effect on blood glucose and insulin levels. However, as mentioned above, other ingredients like flour and fat still add calories, so the total amount of calories and carbohydrate in sugar-free foods may not be much different than the sugar-sweetened versions.

Be aware, too, that sugar alcohols can cause bloating, gas, and have a laxative effect if too much is eaten. On the other hand, sugar substitutes like aspartame (NutraSweet or Equal), saccharin (Sweet'n Low), acesulfame-K (Sunnette), and sucralose (Splenda) do not add a significant number of calories to foods or cause a laxative effect.

Chosen carefully, you will find that some sugar-free products—like sodas, gelatin, pudding, yogurt, hot cocoa mix, and some brands of frozen Fudgesicles and Popsicles—can be a real boon to the carb counter. On the other hand, sugar-free cookies, cakes, and candies often save few or no calories and may still be quite high in carbohydrate. The bottom line is buyer beware—always read labels to be sure a product is the right fit for your diet.

Cinnamon-Mocha Crisps

YIELD: 45 COOKIES

½ cup margarine or butter

⅔ cup sugar

Sugar substitute equal to ¼ cup sugar

¼ cup molasses

¼ cup fat-free egg substitute

1 teaspoon vanilla extract

¾ teaspoon instant coffee granules

1½ cups whole-wheat pastry flour

⅔ cup oat bran

¼ cup plus 2 tablespoons cocoa powder
   (preferably Dutch-processed cocoa)

¾ teaspoon baking soda

½ teaspoon ground cinnamon

¾ cup sliced almonds, finely crushed
   (optional)

1. Place the margarine, sugar, and sugar substitute in a medium bowl and beat until smooth. Beat in the molasses, egg substitute, vanilla, and coffee granules.

2. In a separate bowl, combine the flour, oat bran, cocoa powder, baking soda, and cinnamon and stir to mix. Add the flour mixture to the margarine mixture and beat to mix well.

3. Place the dough in the freezer for about 20 minutes, or until firm enough to handle, then roll the dough into 1-inch balls. If desired, roll the balls in the almonds, coating all sides. Arrange the cookies 1½ inches apart on a nonstick baking sheet. Flatten the cookies to ¼-inch thickness with the bottom of a glass. (If you did not coat the cookies with almonds, dip the bottom of the glass lightly in sugar between cookies to prevent sticking.)

4. Bake at 350 degrees for about 10 to 12 minutes, or until golden brown. Cool on the pan for a couple of minutes, then transfer to wire racks to cool completely. Store in an airtight container.

Nutritional Facts (per cookie)

Calories: 50   *Carbohydrates:* 8.5g   *Cholesterol:* 0mg   *Fat:* 1.8g   *Sat Fat:* 0.5g
Fiber: 1g   *Protein:* 1g   *Sodium:* 40mg   *Calcium:* 5mg
   Diabetic exchanges: ½ carbohydrate, ⅓ fat

Crunchy Peanut-Butter Cookies

YIELD: 45 COOKIES

¾ cup plus 2 tablespoons smooth peanut
butter

¾ cup light brown sugar

Sugar substitute equal to ⅓ cup sugar

¼ cup canola oil

¼ cup fat-free egg substitute

2 tablespoons applesauce

1½ teaspoons vanilla extract

1¼ cups whole-wheat pastry flour

½ cup quick-cooking (1-minute) oats or
oat bran

¾ teaspoon baking soda

1. Preheat the oven to 350 degrees.
2. Place the peanut butter, brown sugar, and sugar substitute in a medium bowl and beat until smooth. Beat in the canola oil, egg substitute, applesauce, and vanilla.
3. In a separate bowl, combine the flour, oats, and baking soda and stir to mix. Add the flour mixture to the peanut-butter mixture and beat to mix well.
4. Roll the dough into 1-inch balls and place 1½ inches apart on a nonstick baking sheet. Flatten each cookie to ¼-inch thickness by crisscrossing with the tines of a fork. (Dip the fork lightly in sugar between cookies to prevent sticking.)
5. Bake for about 10 minutes, or until golden brown. Cool on the pan for a couple of minutes, then transfer to wire racks to cool completely. Store in an airtight container.

Nutritional Facts (per cookie)

Calories: 70   *Carbohydrates:* 8g   *Cholesterol:* 0mg   *Fat:* 3.9g   *Sat Fat:* 0.6g

Fiber: 0.9g   *Protein:* 2g   *Sodium:* 48mg   *Calcium:* 6mg

Diabetic exchanges: ½ carbohydrate, ½ fat

Hamantaschen

FILLING

1¼ cups finely chopped dried apricots,
  prunes, or other dried fruit

1 cup water

2 tablespoons honey

GLAZE

2 tablespoons fat-free egg substitute

1 teaspoon water

PASTRY

¼ cup plus 2 tablespoons margarine
  or butter

¼ cup plus 2 tablespoons sugar

Sugar substitute equal to ¼ cup sugar

¼ cup plus 2 tablespoons fat-free egg
  substitute

1¼ cups unbleached flour

1¼ cups whole-wheat pastry flour

1½ teaspoons baking powder

1. To make the filling, place the dried fruit, water, and honey in a small pot and bring to a boil. Reduce the heat to low, cover, and simmer for about 20 minutes, or until the liquid is absorbed. Set aside to cool to room temperature.

2. To make the glaze, combine the egg substitute and water in a small dish and stir to mix. Set aside.

3. To make the pastry, place the margarine or butter, sugar, and sugar substitute in a medium bowl and beat to mix well. Beat in the egg substitute. In a separate bowl, combine the flours and baking powder and mix well. Add the flour mixture to the margarine mixture and beat until the dough forms a ball.

4. Place a fourth of the dough on a lightly floured surface and roll into a 9-inch circle about ¹⁄₁₆-inch thick. Use a 2¾-inch round cookie cutter or the rim of a glass to cut out rounds of dough. Repeat with the remaining dough and re-roll the scraps as needed to use up all of the dough.

5. Brush a small amount of glaze around the outer edges of each circle. Place 1 teaspoon of filling in the center of each round and fold up 3 sides of each circle about ½ inch to form a tricorn—a 3-sided hat. (Use a spatula to lift the dough circles from the surface to prevent tearing).

6. Place the cookies on a nonstick baking sheet and brush each one with some of the glaze. Repeat with the remaining dough to make 45 cookies.

7. Bake at 350 degrees for about 15 minutes, or until golden brown. Transfer the cookies to wire racks to cool. Store in an airtight container.

Nutritional Facts (per cookie)

Calories: 53   *Carbohydrates:* 10g   *Cholesterol:* 0mg   *Fat:* 1.3g   *Sat Fat:* 0.3g

Fiber: 0.8g   *Protein:* 1.2g   *Sodium:* 34mg   *Calcium:* 11mg

Diabetic exchanges: ½ carbohydrate

∴ Dutch Chocolate Pinwheels ∴

YIELD: 56 COOKIES

½ cup margarine or butter

1 cup plus 2 tablespoons sugar

3 tablespoons fat-free egg substitute

1½ teaspoons vanilla extract

1 cup plus 2 tablespoons unbleached flour

1 cup plus 2 tablespoons oat flour

½ teaspoon baking soda

3 tablespoons Dutch-processed cocoa powder

1 tablespoon plus one 1 teaspoon light (reduced-sugar) chocolate syrup

1. Place the margarine or butter and the sugar in a large bowl and beat with an electric mixer until smooth. Add the egg substitute and vanilla extract and beat to mix well.

2. In a separate bowl, combine the flours and baking soda and stir to mix. Add the flour mixture to the margarine mixture and beat to mix well.

3. Remove half of the dough and set aside. Add the cocoa and chocolate syrup to the remaining dough and beat to mix well.

4. Cut an 18-inch piece of waxed paper and place the white dough on the sheet. Pat the dough into a rectangle about 3 by 7 inches (Note: If the dough seems too sticky to work with, place it in the freezer for a few minutes). Top with another

piece of waxed paper and use a rolling pin to roll the dough into a 6-by-14-inch rectangle. Next, roll the chocolate dough out in the same manner.

5. Peel the waxed paper off the rectangles of dough and lay the chocolate rectangle on top of the white rectangle. Roll the double layer of dough up from the long end, jelly-roll style. Cut the roll in half (for easier handling), wrap each half in waxed paper and freeze for at least 3 hours, or until ready to bake.

6. When ready to bake, slice the dough into ¼-inch thick pieces and arrange on a nonstick baking sheet, spacing them 1½ inches apart.

7. Bake at 350 degrees for about 7 to 9 minutes, or until lightly browned around the edges. Cool the cookies on the pan for 1 minute, then transfer to wire racks to cool completely. Store in an airtight container.

Nutritional Facts (per cookie)
Calories: 46   *Carbohydrates:* 8g   *Cholesterol:* 0mg   *Fat:* 1.5g   *Sat Fat:* 0.4g
Fiber: 0.4g   *Protein:* 0.7g   *Sodium:* 30mg   *Calcium:* 2mg
Diabetic exchanges: ½ carbohydrate, ⅓ fat

Cinnamon Pinwheels

YIELD: 56 COOKIES

½ cup margarine or butter

1 cup plus 2 tablespoons sugar

¼ cup fat-free egg substitute

1½ teaspoons vanilla extract

1 cup plus 2 tablespoons unbleached flour

1 cup plus 2 tablespoons oat flour

¾ teaspoon dried lemon or orange rind

½ teaspoon baking soda

FILLING

1 tablespoon sugar

1 to 1½ teaspoons ground cinnamon

1. Place the margarine or butter and the sugar in a large bowl and beat with an electric mixer until smooth. Add 3 tablespoons of the egg substitute and all of vanilla extract and beat to mix well.

2. In a separate bowl, combine the flours, lemon rind, and baking soda and stir to mix. Add the flour mixture to the margarine mixture and beat to mix well.

3. Cut an 18-inch piece of waxed paper and place half of the dough on the sheet. Pat the dough into a rectangle about 4 by 7 inches (Note: If the dough seems too sticky to work with, place it in the freezer for a few minutes). Top with another piece of waxed paper and use a rolling pin to roll the dough into an 8-by-14-inch rectangle.

4. Peel the waxed paper off the dough. Mix the remaining tablespoon of egg substitute with 1 teaspoon of water and brush over the dough. Combine the sugar and cinnamon, sprinkle the mixture evenly over the dough and roll the dough up jelly-roll style. Cut the roll in half (for easier handling), wrap each half in waxed paper, and freeze for at least 3 hours, or until ready to bake.

5. When ready to bake, slice the dough into ¼-inch-thick pieces and arrange on a nonstick baking sheet, spacing them 1½ inches apart.

6. Bake at 350 degrees for about 7 to 9 minutes, or until lightly browned around the edges. Cool the cookies on the pan for 1 minute, then transfer to wire racks to cool completely. Store in an airtight container.

Nutritional Facts (per cookie)

Calories: 44   *Carbohydrates:* 8g   *Cholesterol:* 0mg   *Fat:* 1.4g   *Sat Fat:* 0.4g
Fiber: 0.3g   *Protein:* 0.7g   *Sodium:* 26mg   *Calcium:* 2mg
   Diabetic exchanges: ½ carbohydrate, ⅓ fat

∵ Pecan Puffs ∵

YIELD: 24 COOKIES

2 large egg whites, warmed to room
   temperature

⅛ teaspoon cream of tartar

⅛ teaspoon salt

¼ cup plus 2 tablespoons sugar

½ teaspoon vanilla extract

½ cup toasted pecans halves (page 25)

1. Preheat the oven to 250 degrees.
2. Place the egg whites in a large bowl and beat at high speed with an electric mixer until foamy. Add the cream of tartar and salt and continue beating until soft peaks form. Still beating, slowly add the sugar, 1 tablespoon at a time, and continue beating until stiff peaks form when the beaters are raised. Beat in the vanilla extract and then fold in the pecans.
3. Line a large baking sheet with aluminum foil. (Do not grease the foil or coat it with cooking spray.) Drop heaping teaspoonfuls of the mixture onto the baking sheet, spacing them 1½ inches apart. Bake for about 45 minutes, or until firm and creamy white. Turn the oven off and let the cookies cool in the oven for 30 minutes with the door closed. Remove the pan from the oven, let the cookies cool to room temperature, and peel them from the foil. Store in an airtight container.

Nutritional Facts (per cookie)

Calories: 29   *Carbohydrates:* 3.5g   *Cholesterol:* 0mg   *Fat:* 1.6g   *Sat Fat:* 0.1g

Fiber: 0.2g   *Protein:* 0.5g   *Sodium:* 17mg   *Calcium:* 2mg

Diabetic exchanges: ¼ carbohydrate

Mint-Chocolate Meringues

YIELD: 24 COOKIES

2 large egg whites, warmed to room temperature

⅛ teaspoon cream of tartar

⅛ teaspoon salt

¼ cup plus 2 tablespoons sugar

1 to 2 tablespoons cocoa powder

¾ teaspoon vanilla extract

½ cup mint chocolate chips

1. Preheat the oven to 250 degrees.
2. Place the egg whites in a large bowl and beat at high speed with an electric mixer until foamy. Add the cream of tartar and salt and continue beating until soft peaks form. Still beating, slowly add the sugar, 1 tablespoon at a time, and continue beat-

ing until stiff peaks form when the beaters are raised. Beat in first the cocoa and then the vanilla extract. Fold in the chocolate chips.

3. Line a large baking sheet with aluminum foil. (Do not grease the foil or coat it with cooking spray.) Drop heaping teaspoonfuls of the mixture onto the baking sheet, spacing them 1½ inches apart. Bake for about 45 minutes, or until firm and creamy white. Turn the oven off and let the cookies cool in the oven for 30 minutes with the door closed. Remove the pan from the oven, let the cookies cool to room temperature, and peel them from the foil. Store in an airtight container.

Nutritional Facts (per cookie)
Calories: 31   *Carbohydrates:* 5.5g   *Cholesterol:* 0mg   *Fat:* 1.1g   *Sat Fat:* 0.6g
Fiber: 0.3g   *Protein:* 0.5g   *Sodium:* 17mg   *Calcium:* 2mg
   Diabetic exchanges: ⅓ carbohydrate

Crispy Chocolate-Nut Cookies

YIELD: 36 COOKIES

¾ cup coarsely chopped dark chocolate or
   semisweet chocolate chips

2 large egg whites, warmed to room
   temperature

¼ teaspoon cream of tartar

Pinch salt

½ cup sugar

½ teaspoon vanilla extract

1 cup chopped almonds, hazelnuts, pecans,
   or walnuts

1. Preheat the oven to 300 degrees.
2. Place the chocolate in the bowl of a food processor and process until coarsely ground. Set aside.
3. Place the egg whites in a large bowl and beat at high speed with an electric mixer until foamy. Add the cream of tartar and salt and continue beating until soft peaks form. Still beating, slowly add the sugar, 1 tablespoon at a time, and continue beating until stiff peaks form when the beaters are raised. Beat in the vanilla extract. Fold in the chocolate and nuts.

4. Line two large baking sheets with aluminum foil and coat with cooking spray. Drop rounded teaspoonfuls of the mixture onto the sheets, spacing them 1½ inches apart. Bake for about 25 minutes, switching the position of the pans after 12 minutes, until the cookies are firm to the touch and lightly browned. Remove the pans from the oven and let the cookies cool for several minutes. Transfer to wire racks to cool completely. Store in an airtight container.

Nutritional Facts (per cookie)

Calories: 44   *Carbohydrates:* 5.5g   *Cholesterol:* 0mg   *Fat:* 2.4g   *Sat Fat:* 0.7g
Fiber: 0.5g   *Protein:* 0.9g   *Sodium:* 7mg   *Calcium:* 8mg
   Diabetic exchanges: ⅓ carbohydrate, ½ fat

Pecan Praline Crisps

YIELD: 36 COOKIES

1½ cups chopped pecans

2 large egg whites, warmed to room
   temperature

Pinch salt

¾ cup light brown sugar

½ teaspoon vanilla extract

36 pecan halves

1. Preheat the oven to 300 degrees.
2. Place the pecans in the bowl of a food processor and process until coarsely ground. Set aside.
3. Place the egg whites in a large bowl and beat at high speed with an electric mixer until foamy. Add the salt and continue beating until soft peaks form. Still beating, slowly add the brown sugar, 1 tablespoon at a time, and continue beating until stiff peaks form when the beaters are raised. Beat in the vanilla extract. Fold in the ground pecans.
4. Line two large baking sheets with aluminum foil (do not coat it with cooking spray). Drop rounded teaspoonfuls of the mixture onto the sheets, spacing them 1½ inches apart. Place a pecan half over the center of each cookie, but do not press

it into the center. Bake for about 18 minutes, switching the position of the pans after 10 minutes, until lightly browned. Remove the pans from the oven and let the cookies cool for several minutes. Transfer to wire racks to cool completely. Store in an airtight container.

Nutritional Facts (per cookie)

Calories: 62   *Carbohydrates:* 5g   *Cholesterol:* 0mg   *Fat:* 4.6g   *Sat Fat:* 0.4g
Fiber: 0.6g   *Protein:* 0.8g   *Sodium:* 9mg   *Calcium:* 8mg
Diabetic exchanges: ⅓ carbohydrate, 1 fat

Cocoa Crunch Biscotti

YIELD: 24 COOKIES

½ cup whole-wheat pastry flour

½ cup oat flour

½ cup cocoa powder (preferably Dutch-processed cocoa)

¼ teaspoon ground cinnamon

¼ teaspoon baking soda

¼ cup margarine or butter

½ cup light brown sugar

Sugar substitute equivalent to ⅓ cup sugar

¼ cup plus 1 tablespoon fat-free egg substitute

1 teaspoon vanilla extract

1 cup chopped walnuts or chopped toasted hazelnuts or pecans (page 25)

1. Place the flours, cocoa, cinnamon, and baking soda in a small bowl and stir to mix well. Set aside.

2. Place the margarine or butter, brown sugar, and sugar substitute in a medium bowl and beat with an electric mixer until smooth. Beat in the egg substitute and vanilla. Add the flour mixture and beat to mix well. Mix in the nuts. Place the dough in the refrigerator for about 10 minutes, or until firm enough to handle.

3. Spray a large baking sheet with nonstick cooking spray. Spray your hands with cooking spray and divide the dough into 2 equal pieces. Shape each piece into a 10-by-2-inch log and lay on the baking sheet.

4. Bake at 350 degrees for about 20 minutes, or until firm to the touch. Cool on the pans for 5 minutes and then transfer the logs to wire racks and cool to room temperature.

5. Using a serrated knife, slice the logs diagonally into ½-inch-thick slices. Arrange the slices standing upright on the baking sheet and bake for about 8 minutes, or until dry and crisp. Cool to room temperature and store in an airtight container.

Nutritional Facts (per cookie)

Calories: 87   *Carbohydrates:* 9g   *Cholesterol:* 0mg   *Fat:* 5.2g   *Sat Fat:* 0.6g

Fiber: 1.4g   *Protein:* 2.6g   *Sodium:* 49mg   *Calcium:* 13mg

Diabetic exchanges: ½ carbohydrate, 1 fat

Poppy Seed-Almond Biscotti

YIELD: 24 COOKIES

¾ cup unbleached flour

¾ cup oat flour

1 teaspoon baking powder

¼ cup margarine or butter

½ cup sugar

Sugar substitute equivalent to ⅓ cup sugar

¼ cup plus 1 tablespoon fat-free egg substitute

1 teaspoon vanilla extract

1 cup chopped or slivered almonds

1 tablespoon poppy seeds

1. Place the flours and baking powder in a small bowl and stir to mix well. Set aside.

2. Place the margarine or butter, sugar, and sugar substitute in a medium bowl and beat with an electric mixer until smooth. Beat in the egg substitute and vanilla. Add the flour mixture and beat to mix well. Mix in the almonds and poppy seeds. Place the dough in the refrigerator for about 10 minutes, or until firm enough to handle.

3. Spray a large baking sheet with nonstick cooking spray. Spray your hands with cooking spray and divide the dough into 2 equal pieces. Shape each piece into a 10-by-2-inch log and lay on the baking sheet.

4. Bake at 350 degrees for about 20 minutes, or until firm to the touch. Cool on the pans for 5 minutes and then transfer the logs to wire racks and cool to room temperature.

5. Using a serrated knife, slice the logs diagonally into ½-inch-thick slices. Arrange the slices standing upright on the baking sheet and bake for about 8 minutes, or until dry and crisp. Cool to room temperature and store in an airtight container.

Nutritional Facts (per cookie)
Calories: 78 *Carbohydrates:* 9g *Cholesterol:* 0mg *Fat:* 3.6g *Sat Fat:* 0.5g
Fiber: 1g *Protein:* 2g *Sodium:* 42mg *Calcium:* 31mg
Diabetic exchanges: ½ carbohydrate, ½ fat

Peanut-Butter Marshmallow Treats

YIELD: 20 BARS

½ cup creamy peanut butter

1 tablespoon water

5 cups miniature marshmallows

5 cups crisp brown rice cereal

1. Coat a 4-quart nonstick pot with cooking spray and add the peanut butter, water, and marshmallows. Cover and cook over low heat without stirring for 3 minutes. Stir the mixture, cover, and continue to cook for about 3 minutes more, stirring after each minute, until the mixture is melted and smooth.

2. Remove the pot from the heat and quickly stir in the cereal. Press the mixture into a 9-by-13-inch nonstick pan. (Place a sheet of waxed paper over the cereal mixture

as you press to prevent sticking.) Cool to room temperature before cutting into squares and serving. To speed the cooling process you can place the pan in the freezer for about 15 minutes, or until the bars are set.

Nutritional Facts (per bar)

Calories: 97   *Carbohydrates:* 16g   *Cholesterol:* 0mg   *Fat:* 3.3g   *Sat Fat:* 0.7g

Fiber: 0.8g   *Protein:* 2.3g   *Sodium:* 94mg   *Calcium:* 3mg

    Diabetic exchanges: 1 carbohydrate, ½ fat

6. Refreshing Frozen Desserts

Cool and refreshing, frozen desserts are everyone's favorite treat on a sizzling summer day. But don't limit these icy confections to the summer months. Elegant and surprisingly simple to make, frozen desserts are perfect for year-round entertaining. And since many of these recipes must be prepared in advance, and can be kept in the freezer until ready to serve, they can be a real boon to the busy cook.

The star ingredients in this chapter's frozen delights make these treats as healthful as they are delicious. Ripe fruits provide a bounty of nutrients as well as great flavor and natural sweetness. And low-fat dairy products such as sugar-free yogurts, low-fat milk, reduced-fat ricotta cheese, and ready-made no-added-sugar ice cream, provide plenty of calcium without excess carbs or calories.

So whether you are looking for a simple frozen fruit pop to take the heat out of a sultry afternoon, a creamy low-carb frozen yogurt for an evening snack, or a show-stopping sundae or fabulous torte, you need look no further. These temptingly sweet treats will prove that smart eating can be ultra-satisfying and incredibly delicious.

Fruitful Frozen Yogurt

1½ cups frozen fruit, coarsely chopped and
 thawed (such as raspberries, strawberries, blueberries, blackberries,
 cherries, or peaches)

4 cups light vanilla yogurt (or use the same
 flavor yogurt as the fruit you choose)

Sugar substitute equal to ¼ cup sugar

1. Place the fruit and the accumulated juices in a large bowl and mash slightly with a fork. Stir in the yogurt and sugar substitute. Pour the mixture into a 1½-quart ice-cream maker and proceed as directed by the manufacturer. (If you don't own an ice-cream maker, see the inset on page 130 for directions for making the dessert in your freezer.)
2. Spoon into dessert dishes and serve immediately.

Nutritional Facts (per ⅞-cup serving)
Calories: 114 *Carbohydrates:* 19g *Cholesterol:* 4mg *Fat:* 0.4g *Sat Fat:* 0.1g
Fiber: 2g *Protein:* 8g *Sodium:* 122mg *Calcium:* 273mg
 Diabetic exchanges: 1 carbohydrate

Cherry Crunch Ice Cream

15 ounces nonfat or reduced-fat ricotta cheese

1 cup nonfat or low-fat milk

4 cups frozen pitted sweet dark cherries, thawed

Sugar substitute equal to ¾ cup sugar

⅓ cup chopped pitted dried sweet cherries
 or coarsely chopped dark chocolate

⅓ cup chopped walnuts or toasted pecans
 (page 25)

1. Place the ricotta, milk, cherries, and sugar substitute in a blender and blend until smooth.

2. Stir in the dried cherries and nuts and pour the mixture into a 1½-quart ice-cream maker. Proceed as directed by the manufacturer. (If you don't own an ice-cream maker, see the inset on page 130 for directions for making the dessert in your freezer.)

3. Spoon into dessert dishes and serve immediately.

Nutritional Facts (per ¾-cup serving)
Calories: 174   *Carbohydrates:* 24g   *Cholesterol:* 2mg   *Fat:* 3.3g   *Sat Fat:* 0.3g
Fiber: 2.8g   *Protein:* 11g   *Sodium:* 68mg   *Calcium:* 317mg
Diabetic exchanges: 1½ carbohydrate, ½ fat

White Chocolate-Chunk Ice Cream

YIELD: 7 SERVINGS

3 cups nonfat or low-fat milk

1 cup nonfat or reduced-fat ricotta cheese

1 package (4-serving size) sugar-free instant white chocolate pudding mix

Sugar substitute equal to ½ cup sugar

⅓ cup chopped toasted pecans or almonds (page 25)

⅓ cup chopped dark chocolate

1. Place the milk and ricotta cheese in a blender and blend until smooth. Add the pudding mix and sugar substitute and blend for 30 seconds more.

2. Stir in the pecans or almonds and chocolate and pour the mixture into a 1½-quart ice-cream maker. Proceed as directed by the manufacturer. (If you don't own an ice-cream maker, see the inset on page 130 for directions for making the dessert in your freezer.)

3. Spoon into dessert dishes and serve immediately.

Nutritional Facts (per ¾-cup serving)
Calories: 167   *Carbohydrates:* 18g   *Cholesterol:* 3mg   *Fat:* 6.6g   *Sat Fat:* 1.9g
Fiber: 1g   *Protein:* 10g   *Sodium:* 254mg   *Calcium:* 307mg
Diabetic exchanges: 1 carbohydrate, 1 fat

Cantaloupe Sunshine Sorbet

4½ cups fresh cantaloupe cubes

¾ cup orange juice

Sugar substitute equal to ⅓ to ½ cup sugar

1. Place all of the ingredients in a blender and blend until smooth.
2. Pour the mixture into a 1½-quart ice-cream maker and proceed as directed by the manufacturer. (If you don't own an ice-cream maker, see the inset on page 130 for directions for making the dessert in your freezer.)
3. Spoon into dessert dishes and serve immediately.

Nutritional Facts (per ¾-cup serving)
Calories: 73   *Carbohydrates:* 17g   *Cholesterol:* 0mg   *Fat:* 0.5g   *Sat Fat:* 0.1g
Fiber: 1.2g   *Protein:* 1.5g   *Sodium:* 13mg   *Calcium:* 20mg
Diabetic exchanges: 1 carbohydrate

Refreshing Apricot Sorbet

YIELD: 7 SERVINGS

2 cans (15 ounces each) apricots packed in juice or light syrup

Sugar substitute equal to ½ to ¾ cup sugar

1. Place the undrained apricots and sugar substitute in a blender and blend until smooth.

2. Pour the mixture into a 1½-quart ice-cream maker and proceed as directed by the manufacturer. (If you don't own an ice-cream maker, see the inset on page 130 for directions for making the dessert in your freezer.)
3. Spoon into dessert dishes and serve immediately.

Nutritional Facts (per ¾-cup serving)
Calories: 63   *Carbohydrates:* 16g   *Cholesterol:* 0mg   *Fat:* 0g   *Sat Fat:* 0g
Fiber: 1.9g   *Protein:* 0.8g   *Sodium:* 5mg   *Calcium:* 15mg
   Diabetic exchanges: 1 carbohydrate

Cinnamon-Mocha Sorbet

YIELD: 6 SERVINGS

1 package (4-serving size) sugar-free instant chocolate pudding mix

¼ cup nonfat dry milk powder

½ teaspoon ground cinnamon

Sugar substitute equal to ½ cup sugar

4 cups nonfat or low-fat milk

¼ cup coffee liqueur

1. Place the pudding mix, milk powder, cinnamon, and sugar substitute in a large bowl and stir to mix. Add half of the milk and beat at low speed with an electric mixer. Add the remaining milk and liqueur and beat for another minute.
2. Pour the mixture into a 1½-quart ice-cream maker and proceed as directed by the manufacturer. (If you don't own an ice-cream maker, see the inset on page 130 for directions for making the dessert in your freezer.)
3. Spoon into dessert dishes and serve immediately.

Nutritional Facts (per ¾-cup serving)
Calories: 137   *Carbohydrates:* 22g   *Cholesterol:* 4mg   *Fat:* 0.4g   *Sat Fat:* 0.2g
Fiber: 0.2g   *Protein:* 7g   *Sodium:* 155mg   *Calcium:* 236mg
   Diabetic exchanges: 1½ carbohydrate

Triple Berry Sorbet

½ cup light (reduced-sugar) cranberry juice cocktail

5 cups frozen strawberries, thawed and undrained

1 cup frozen raspberries, thawed and undrained

Sugar substitute equal to ½ to ¾ cup sugar

¼ cup raspberry liqueur (optional)

1. Place all of the ingredients in a blender and blend until smooth.
2. Pour the mixture into a 1½-quart ice-cream maker and proceed as directed by the manufacturer. (If you don't own an ice-cream maker, see the inset on page 130 for directions for making the dessert in your freezer.)
3. Spoon into dessert dishes and serve immediately.

Nutritional Facts (per ¾-cup serving)
Calories: 63   *Carbohydrates:* 15g   *Cholesterol:* 0mg   *Fat:* 0.6g   *Sat Fat:* 0g
Fiber: 4.6g   *Protein:* 1g   *Sodium:* 2mg   *Calcium:* 26mg
Diabetic exchanges: 1 carbohydrate

Mango-Orange Ice

YIELD: 5 SERVINGS

2 cups orange juice

1½ cups peeled and diced mango (about 1 large)

Sugar substitute equal to ½ cup sugar

1. Place all of the ingredients in a blender and blend until smooth. Pour the mixture into an 8-inch square pan.
2. Place the pan in the freezer and freeze for 30 minutes, or until ice crystals begin to form around the sides of the pan. Using a fork, stir the frozen crystals from around the edges of the pan back into the liquid portion.

3. Repeat this scraping process every 20 minutes for about 2 hours, or until the mixture is icy and granular. Spoon the ice into five 8-ounce dessert dishes or wine glasses and serve immediately.

Nutritional Facts (per ¾-cup serving)
Calories: 77   *Carbohydrates:* 19g   *Cholesterol:* 0mg   *Fat:* 0.3g   *Sat Fat:* 0g
Fiber: 1.1g   *Protein:* 1g   *Sodium:* 2mg   *Calcium:* 16mg
   Diabetic exchanges: 1 carbohydrate

Making Ice Cream, Sherbet, Sorbet, and Frozen Yogurt in Your Freezer

An ice-cream maker will produce the smoothest, creamiest light ice creams, sherbets, and sorbets imaginable. Inexpensive machines that do not require any salt, ice, or even electricity are widely available. These machines are convenient to have on hand if you plan on making your own frozen desserts on a regular basis. However, if you don't have an ice-cream maker, you can still enjoy frozen treats by using the following steps to prepare them in your freezer.

1. Prepare the ice-cream, sorbet, yogurt, or sherbet mixture as directed in the recipe, but instead of transferring the mixture to an ice-cream maker, pour it into an 8-inch square pan. Cover the pan with aluminum foil and place it in the freezer for several hours or until the outer 2-inch edge of the mixture is frozen. If you prefer, you can prepare the mixture a few days ahead of time. Then remove it from the freezer and let it sit at room temperature for about 20 minutes or until thawed enough to break into chunks, before proceeding with step 2.
2. Break the mixture into chunks and place in the bowl of a food processor. Process for several minutes, or until light, creamy, and smooth. Depending on the capacity of your machine, you may have to do this in two batches.
3. Return the mixture to the freezer and freeze for at least 2 hours, or until firm. About 20 minutes before serving, remove the dessert from the freezer and allow it to soften slightly at room temperature. Scoop into dessert dishes and serve immediately.

Very Cranberry Ice

YIELD: 6 SERVINGS

3¼ cups light (reduced-sugar) cranberry juice cocktail

¾ cup whole-berry cranberry sauce

1. Place the cranberry juice and cranberry sauce in a blender and blend until the cranberries are pulverized into small bits. Pour the mixture into an 8-inch square pan.
2. Place the pan in the freezer and freeze for 30 minutes, or until ice crystals begin to form around the sides of the pan. Using a fork, stir the frozen crystals from around the edges of the pan back into the liquid portion.
3. Repeat this scraping process every 20 minutes for about 2 hours, or until the mixture is icy and granular. Spoon the ice into five 8-ounce dessert dishes or wine glasses and serve immediately. Or freeze for later use. Let the pan sit at room temperature for about 20 minutes before serving.

Nutritional Facts (per ¾-cup serving)
Calories: 83   *Carbohydrates:* 21g   *Cholesterol:* 0mg   *Fat:* 0g   *Sat Fat:* 0g
Fiber: 0.5g   *Protein:* 0g   *Sodium:* 14mg   *Calcium:* 12mg
Diabetic exchanges: 1½ carbohydrate

Almond Crunch Ice-Cream Balls

YIELD: 6 SERVINGS

4 cups low-fat or light no-added-sugar vanilla ice cream,
*   slightly softened*

⅔ cup sliced toasted almonds (page 25)

½ cup light (reduced-sugar) chocolate syrup

1. Using an ice-cream scoop, shape ⅔-cup portions of the ice cream into 6 balls. Place the balls in a single layer in a covered container and freeze for at least 1 hour, or until the outside of the balls are firm.

2. Remove the balls from the freezer and roll each ball in the almonds, turning to coat all sides and pressing the almonds onto the ice cream to make them stick. Return the coated ice-cream balls to the freezer and freeze for at least 2 hours, or until firm.

3. To serve, place one ice-cream ball in each of six dessert dishes. Drizzle 1 tablespoon plus 1 teaspoon of the chocolate syrup over the top of each dessert and serve immediately.

Nutritional Facts (per serving)
Calories: 233 *Carbohydrates:* 33g *Cholesterol:* 13mg *Fat:* 8.5g *Sat Fat:* 1.8g
Fiber: 2.5g *Protein:* 7.2g *Sodium:* 99mg *Calcium:* 158mg
Diabetic exchanges: 2 carbohydrate, 1½ fat

Variation: Pecan Crunch Ice-Cream Balls

Substitute chopped toasted pecans for the almonds and Honey-Orange Sauce (page 88) for the light chocolate syrup.

Nutritional Facts (per serving)
Calories: 250 *Carbohydrates:* 31g *Cholesterol:* 13mg *Fat:* 12g *Sat Fat:* 2.1g
Fiber: 2.6g *Protein:* 5.2g *Sodium:* 73mg *Calcium:* 144mg
Diabetic exchanges: 2 carbohydrate, 2 fat

Variation: Walnut Crunch Ice-Cream Balls

Substitute chopped walnuts for the almonds and Really Raspberry Sauce (page 55) for the light chocolate syrup.

Nutritional Facts (per serving)
Calories: 235 *Carbohydrates:* 27g *Cholesterol:* 13mg *Fat:* 11.3g *Sat Fat:* 2.1g
Fiber: 2.8g *Protein:* 6g *Sodium:* 74mg *Calcium:* 150mg
Diabetic exchanges: 2 carbohydrate, 2 fat

Light Ice-Cream Sandwiches

8 large (2½-by-5-inch) reduced-fat chocolate graham crackers

2 cups no-added-sugar low-fat or light ice cream, any flavor, slightly softened

1. Break each graham cracker in half so that you have 16 squares, each measuring 2½ by 2½ inches.
2. Spread ¼ cup of the ice cream over 1 square, top with another square, and press the crackers together. Smooth the edges of the ice cream with a knife.
3. Wrap the sandwich in plastic wrap and place in the freezer. Repeat with the remaining ingredients to make 8 sandwiches. Freeze for at least 1 hour before serving.

Nutritional Facts (per serving)
Calories: 105   *Carbohydrates:* 19g   *Cholesterol:* 5mg   *Fat:* 1.8g   *Sat Fat:* 0.5g
Fiber: 0.7g   *Protein:* 2.5g   *Sodium:* 127mg   *Calcium:* 50mg
Diabetic exchanges: 1 carbohydrate, ½ fat

Strawberry Crunch Parfaits

1 cup sliced fresh strawberries

Sugar substitute equal to 1 tablespoon sugar

½ cup low-fat granola cereal

2 cups no-added-sugar low-fat or light ice cream

1. Place the strawberries and sugar substitute in a small bowl and toss to mix.
2. To assemble the desserts, place 2 tablespoons of berries in the bottom of each of

four 8-ounce balloon wine glasses. Top with ¼ cup of ice cream and 1 tablespoon of the granola. Repeat the layers and serve immediately.

Nutritional Facts (per serving)
Calories: 157   *Carbohydrates:* 29g   *Cholesterol:* 10mg   *Fat:* 2.9g   *Sat Fat:* 1g
Fiber: 2.7g   *Protein:* 4.4g   *Sodium:* 78mg   *Calcium:* 106mg
Diabetic exchanges: 2 carbohydrate, ½ fat

Peach Melba Sundaes

YIELD: 4 SERVINGS

1½ cups frozen unsweetened raspberries, thawed

Sugar substitute equal to 2 tablespoons sugar

1 cup sliced fresh peaches or canned sliced peaches in juice, drained

2 cups no-added-sugar low-fat or light vanilla ice cream

1. Press the raspberries through a wire strainer and into a small bowl to remove the seeds. Stir in the sugar substitute. Set aside.
2. Place a ½–cup scoop of ice cream in each of 4 dessert dishes and arrange a quarter of the peach slices around the ice cream in each dish. Top each serving with some of the raspberry sauce. Serve immediately.

Nutritional Facts (per serving)
Calories: 133   *Carbohydrates:* 25g   *Cholesterol:* 10mg   *Fat:* 2.1g   *Sat Fat:* 1g
Fiber: 2.2g   *Protein:* 3.5g   *Sodium:* 60mg   *Calcium:* 107mg
Diabetic exchanges: 1½ carbohydrate, ½ fat

Sundaes with Cherry-Brandy Sauce

YIELD: 4 SERVINGS

1 teaspoon cornstarch

3 tablespoons orange juice

2 cups coarsely chopped fresh or frozen dark
sweet pitted cherries

2 tablespoons brandy

Sugar substitute equal to 2 tablespoons
sugar

2 cups low-fat or light no-added-sugar
vanilla ice cream

¼ cup chopped toasted pecans (page 25)
or chopped walnuts

1. To make the sauce, place the cornstarch in a small bowl, add 1 tablespoon of the orange juice, and stir to dissolve the cornstarch. Set aside.

2. Place the cherries and remaining orange juice in a small pot and place over medium heat. Cover and cook for several minutes or until the cherries soften and release their juices. Add the brandy and sugar substitute and stir to mix well. Add the cornstarch mixture and cook for a minute or two, or until the mixture thickens.

3. Place a ½-cup scoop of ice cream in each of 4 dessert dishes. Top the ice cream in each dish with a quarter of the warm sauce and a sprinkling of the nuts. Serve immediately.

Nutritional Facts (per serving)
Calories: 234   Carbohydrates: 33g   Cholesterol: 10mg   Fat: 7.3g   Sat Fat: 1.5g
Fiber: 3.7g   Protein: 4.4g   Sodium: 55mg   Calcium: 114mg
Diabetic exchanges: 2 carbohydrate, 1½ fat

Frozen Chocolate & Peanut-Butter Torte

6 sugar-free cream-filled chocolate
    sandwich cookies, coarsely crushed

¼ cup peanut butter

Sugar substitute equal to 1 tablespoon sugar

⅓ cup nonfat or low-fat milk

2 cups low-fat or light no-added-sugar
    chocolate ice cream, slightly softened

2 cups low-fat or light no-added-sugar
    vanilla ice cream, slightly softened

1. Spread the cookies evenly over the bottom of an 8-by-4-inch pan. Place the peanut butter and sugar substitute in a small bowl and slowly add the milk, whisking until smooth. Add a little more milk if needed to bring the mixture to a thick pouring consistency. Drizzle the mixture over the cookies and place the pan in the freezer for about 20 minutes, or until the peanut-butter mixture is firm.

2. Spoon the chocolate ice cream evenly over the peanut-butter layer. Cover the pan and freeze for at least 1 hour. Spread the vanilla ice cream over the chocolate ice cream layer. Cover and freeze for several hours, or until firm.

3. When ready to serve, cut the dessert into 1-inch slices, place on serving plates, and let sit for about 10 minutes at room temperature before serving.

Nutritional Facts (per serving)
Calories: 183   *Carbohydrates:* 25g   *Cholesterol:* 10mg   *Fat:* 7.5g   *Sat Fat:* 1.9g
Fiber: 1.8g   *Protein:* 6g   *Sodium:* 123mg   *Calcium:* 123mg
   Diabetic exchanges: 1½ carbohydrate, 1½ fat

136 · Diabetic Dream Desserts

Frozen Chocolate-Raspberry Torte

6 sugar-free cream-filled chocolate sandwich cookies, coarsely crushed

1 cup frozen raspberries, thawed

3 tablespoons Chambord or raspberry liqueur

Sugar substitute equal to 2 tablespoons sugar

2 cups low-fat or light no-added-sugar chocolate ice cream, slightly softened

2 cups low-fat or light no-added-sugar vanilla ice cream, slightly softened

⅓ cup sliced almonds (optional)

1. Spread the cookies evenly over the bottom of an 8-by-4-inch pan. Place the raspberries and the juices that have accumulated, liqueur, and sugar substitute in a mini food processor and process until smooth. Spread the mixture over the cookies and place the pan in the freezer for about 20 minutes, or until the firm to the touch.
2. Spoon the chocolate ice cream evenly over the raspberry layer. Cover the pan and freeze for at least 1 hour. Spread the vanilla ice cream over the chocolate ice cream layer. Sprinkle the almonds over the top if desired. Cover and freeze for several hours, or until firm.
3. When ready to serve, cut the dessert into 1-inch slices, place on serving plates, and let sit for about 10 minutes at room temperature before serving.

Nutritional Facts (per serving)
Calories: 162   *Carbohydrates:* 27g   *Cholesterol:* 10mg   *Fat:* 3.6g   *Sat Fat:* 1.4g
Fiber: 2.3g   *Protein:* 3.6g   *Sodium:* 98mg   *Calcium:* 108mg
  Diabetic exchanges: 2 carbohydrate, 1 fat

Frozen Cappuccino Torte

YIELD: 8 SERVINGS

6 ladyfingers, split open

2 tablespoons coffee liqueur

2 cups low-fat or light no-added-sugar
cappuccino ice cream, slightly softened

⅓ cup sliced almonds

⅓ cup chopped dark chocolate

2 cups low-fat or light no-added-sugar
vanilla ice cream, slightly softened

1. Spread the ladyfingers, split side up, over the bottom of an 8-by-4-inch pan. Drizzle the liqueur over the ladyfingers. Spread the cappuccino ice cream over the ladyfingers. Combine the almonds and chocolate and sprinkle half of the mixture over the cappuccino ice cream. Cover the pan and freeze for at least 1 hour.

2. Spread the vanilla ice cream over the cappuccino layer and sprinkle the remaining almonds and chocolate over the top. Cover and freeze for several hours, or until firm.

3. When ready to serve, cut the dessert into 1-inch slices, place on serving plates, and let sit for about 10 minutes at room temperature before serving.

Nutritional Facts (per serving)
Calories: 186   *Carbohydrates:* 27g   *Cholesterol:* 19mg   *Fat:* 6.1g   *Sat Fat:* 2.5g
Fiber: 1.9g   *Protein:* 4.5g   *Sodium:* 94mg   *Calcium:* 117mg
Diabetic exchanges: 2 carbohydrate, 1 fat

Berries and Cream Cake

YIELD: 12 SERVINGS

1 angel food cake (about 14 ounces)

3 cups no-added-sugar low-fat or light
vanilla or raspberry-ripple ice cream,
slightly softened

3 cups sliced fresh strawberries

1½ cups fresh blueberries or
blackberries

1. Using a serrated knife, cut a 1½-inch-deep channel in the top of the cake, leaving ⅜ inch of the cake intact on either side of the channel. (Reserve the cut-out cake for another use.) Spoon the ice cream evenly into the hollowed-out section of the cake. Wrap the cake in plastic wrap and freeze for at least 2 hours, or until ready to serve.

2. When ready to serve, remove the cake from the freezer and unwrap. Place the cake in the center of a 12-inch round serving platter.

3. Toss the berries together and arrange 1½ cups of the mixture over the top of the cake, covering the channel. Arrange the remaining fruit around the base of the cake. Slice and serve immediately.

Nutritional Facts (per serving)
Calories: 139   *Carbohydrates:* 29g   *Cholesterol:* 5mg   *Fat:* 1.4g   *Sat Fat:* 0.5g
Fiber: 2.3g   *Protein:* 3.4g   *Sodium:* 223mg   *Calcium:* 93mg
   Diabetic exchanges: 2 carbohydrate

Selecting the Best Ice Cream

Countless brands of "sugar-free" and "no-added-sugar" brands of ice cream are now available to choose from. These products are typically sweetened with a combination of sugar alcohols and artificial sweeteners and have 25 to 50 percent fewer carbs than regular ice cream. The caveat is many of these products are loaded with saturated fat and save you few or no calories.

What should you look for when buying ice cream? First, go for a low-fat or light brand, as this will limit your intake of artery-clogging saturated fat. Next, compare calories and carbohydrates and choose a brand that is moderate in both. And realize that no ice cream is totally sugar-free because some sugar (lactose) is naturally present in the milk that ice cream is made from.

Sensational Strawberry Pops

4 cups coarsely chopped frozen strawberries

¼ cup plus 2 tablespoons frozen white grape or cranberry juice
  concentrate, thawed

Sugar substitute equal to ¼ cup sugar

1. Let the berries sit at room temperature for about 15 minutes, or until they are partially thawed.

2. Place the berries, juice concentrate, and sugar substitute in a food processor and process until smooth. If preferred, leave the mixture a little chunky.

3. Spoon the mixture into eight 2½-ounce Popsicle molds or 2½-ounce paper cups. If using molds, insert the sticks and freeze for several hours or until firm. If using paper cups, let the pops partially freeze before inserting a Popsicle stick in the center of each.

4. To serve, remove from the freezer and let stand at room temperature for several minutes before unmolding.

Nutritional Facts (per pop)
Calories: 52   *Carbohydrates:* 12g   *Cholesterol:* 0mg   *Fat:* 0.4g   *Sat Fat:* 0.1g
Fiber: 2g   *Protein:* 0.8g   *Sodium:* 4mg   *Calcium:* 18mg
   Diabetic exchanges: 1 carbohydrate

Frozen Yogurt Fruit Pops

YIELD: 10 POPS

2 cups frozen strawberries, peaches, blueberries, cherries, or bananas

2 cups light vanilla yogurt

Sugar substitute equal to 3 to 4 tablespoons sugar

1. Place all of the ingredients in a food processor and process until smooth. If preferred, leave the mixture a little chunky.
2. Spoon the mixture into ten 2½-ounce Popsicle molds or 2½-ounce paper cups. If using molds, insert the sticks and freeze for several hours, or until firm. If using paper cups, let the Popsicles partially freeze before inserting a Popsicle stick in the center of each.
3. To serve, remove from the freezer and let stand at room temperature for several minutes before unmolding.

Nutritional Facts (per pop)
Calories: 49   *Carbohydrates:* 9g   *Cholesterol:* 1mg   *Fat:* 0.2g   *Sat Fat:* 0g
Fiber: 1.5g   *Protein:* 3g   *Sodium:* 37mg   *Calcium:* 89mg
   Diabetic exchanges: ½ carbohydrate

7. Fabulous Fruit Desserts

From a nutritional standpoint, it's hard to beat fruit-based desserts. For one thing, fruit desserts are some of the easiest to make with little or no added sugar. For another, these treats can provide a respectable amount of nutrition. And from a pure pleasure standpoint, fruit desserts—from bubbling crisps and cobblers to elegant liqueur-laced delights—frequently top the list of all-time favorites.

This chapter presents a stellar selection of tempting fruit desserts made the light and healthy way. And as you will see, by using the right ingredients, it's easy to reduce sugar and fat and boost nutrition without sacrificing the flavors you love. The recipes in this chapter start with a variety of naturally sweet fresh, frozen, and canned fruits. Ingredients like whole-grain oats, wheat germ, and nuts star in delightfully crisp and crunchy toppings. And a dash of cinnamon, nutmeg, and other sweet spices brings out the delicious flavors of these dishes. So whether you are looking for something cool and refreshing or warm, bubbly, and full of down-home goodness, here you will find a fabulous selection of desserts that are destined to become family favorites.

Peach-Almond Crisp

2 cans (15 ounces each) sliced peaches
   in juice

2½ teaspoons cornstarch

Sugar substitute equal to ¼ cup sugar

¼ teaspoon ground cinnamon

¼ teaspoon ground nutmeg

TOPPING

2 cups oat-flake-and-almond cereal

¼ cup light brown sugar

2 tablespoons soft reduced-fat margarine or
   3 tablespoons soft regular margarine

⅓ cup sliced almonds

1. Preheat the oven to 375 degrees.

2. Drain the peaches, reserving ½ cup of the juice, and cut into 1-inch pieces. Place 1 tablespoon of the juice in a 2-quart pot, add the cornstarch, and stir to dissolve the cornstarch. Add the sugar substitute, cinnamon, nutmeg, and remaining juice and stir to mix well. Place the pot over medium heat and cook, stirring constantly, for a couple of minutes, or until the mixture is thickened and bubbly. Stir in the drained peaches and set aside.

3. To make the topping, place the cereal and brown sugar in a food processor and process into coarse crumbs. Add the margarine and process for a few seconds more, or until the mixture is moist and crumbly. Stir in the almonds.

4. Sprinkle the topping over the fruit and bake uncovered for about 20 minutes, or until the filling is bubbly around the edges and the topping is golden brown. Let sit for 20 minutes before serving.

Nutritional Facts (per serving)

Calories: 158 Carbohydrates: 29g Cholesterol: 0mg Fat: 4.4g Sat Fat: 0.7g

Fiber: 2.5g Protein: 2.7g Sodium: 93mg Calcium: 29mg

  Diabetic exchanges: 2 carbohydrate, 1 fat

Chocolate-Cherry Crisp

2 cans (20 ounces each) sugar-free or light (reduced-sugar) cherry pie filling

TOPPING
½ cup oat bran
⅓ cup light brown sugar
2 tablespoons Dutch-processed cocoa powder

½ teaspoon ground cinnamon
2 tablespoons soft margarine, brought to room temperature
1 tablespoon light (reduced-sugar) chocolate syrup
½ cup chopped walnuts

1. Preheat the oven to 375 degrees.
2. Coat a 9-inch pie pan with cooking spray and spread the pie filling evenly in the dish.
3. To make the topping, place the oat bran, brown sugar, cocoa powder, and cinnamon in a medium bowl and stir to mix well. Add the margarine and chocolate syrup and stir until the mixture is moist and crumbly. Stir in the walnuts.
4. Sprinkle the topping over the fruit and bake uncovered for about 25 minutes, or until the filling is bubbly around the edges and the topping begins to brown. Let sit for 20 minutes before serving.

Nutritional Facts (per serving)
Calories: 180   *Carbohydrates:* 28g   *Cholesterol:* 0mg   *Fat:* 7.2g   *Sat Fat:* 1.1g
Fiber: 2.5g   *Protein:* 3.2g   *Sodium:* 53mg   *Calcium:* 18mg
Diabetic exchanges: 2 carbohydrate, 1½ fat

Plum-Delicious Crisp

5 cups sliced fresh unpeeled plums

Sugar substitute equal to ¼ cup plus
  2 tablespoons sugar

1 tablespoon cornstarch

TOPPING

¾ cup quick-cooking (1-minute) oats

⅓ cup light brown sugar

½ teaspoon ground cinnamon

1 tablespoon soft margarine

1 tablespoon frozen (thawed) white
  grape juice concentrate or
  maple syrup

½ cup chopped walnuts or
  pecans

1. Preheat the oven to 375 degrees.
2. Place the plums, sugar substitute, and cornstarch in a large bowl and toss to mix well. Coat a 9-inch pie pan with cooking spray and spread the plum mixture evenly in the dish. Cover the dish with aluminum foil and bake for 15 minutes.
3. To make the topping, place the oats, brown sugar, and cinnamon in a medium bowl and stir to mix well. Add the margarine and juice concentrate or maple syrup and stir until the mixture is moist and crumbly. Stir in the nuts.
4. Sprinkle the topping over the fruit and bake uncovered for about 20 minutes, or until the filling is bubbly around the edges and the topping is golden brown. Let sit for 20 minutes before serving.

Nutritional Facts (per serving)
Calories: 180   *Carbohydrates:* 29g   *Cholesterol:* 0mg   *Fat:* 6.6g   *Sat Fat:* 0.7g
Fiber: 2.7g   *Protein:* 3.9g   *Sodium:* 14mg   *Calcium:* 18mg
  Diabetic exchanges: 2 carbohydrate, 1 fat

Apple-Raisin Crisp

6 cups sliced peeled apples

Sugar substitute equal to ⅓ cup sugar

1 tablespoon cornstarch

¼ teaspoon ground cinnamon

¼ teaspoon ground nutmeg

¼ cup dark raisins

¼ cup apple juice

TOPPING

½ cup old-fashioned (5-minute) rolled oats

3 tablespoons whole-wheat pastry flour

¼ cup plus 2 tablespoons light brown sugar

½ teaspoon ground cinnamon

¼ teaspoon ground nutmeg

2 tablespoons soft reduced-fat margarine or
   3 tablespoons soft regular margarine

½ cup chopped pecans or walnuts

1. Preheat the oven to 375 degrees.
2. Place the apples, sugar substitute, cornstarch, cinnamon, and nutmeg in a large bowl and toss to mix. Add the raisins and apple juice and toss again. Coat a 9-inch deep-dish pie pan with cooking spray and spread the mixture in the pan. Cover the pan with aluminum foil and bake for 25 minutes.
3. To make the topping, place the oats, whole-wheat flour, brown sugar, cinnamon, and nutmeg in a medium bowl and stir to mix. Add the margarine and stir until the mixture is moist and crumbly. Stir in the nuts.
4. Sprinkle the topping over the fruit mixture and bake uncovered for an additional 20 minutes, or until the fruit is bubbly and the topping is golden brown. Let sit for at least 20 minutes before serving.

Nutritional Facts (per serving)

Calories: 199   Carbohydrates: 34g   Cholesterol: 0mg   Fat: 7.2g   Sat Fat: 0.9g

Fiber: 3.5g   Protein: 2.1g   Sodium: 31mg   Calcium: 22mg

Diabetic exchanges: 2 carbohydrate, 1½ fat

Mixed-Fruit Crisp

YIELD: 8 SERVINGS

15-ounce can sliced peaches or apricots
    in juice

15-ounce can sliced pears in juice

2½ teaspoons cornstarch

Sugar substitute equal to ¼ cup sugar

¼ teaspoon ground cinnamon

¼ teaspoon ground nutmeg

TOPPING

½ cup old-fashioned (5-minute) oats

¼ cup toasted wheat germ

⅓ cup light brown sugar

½ teaspoon ground cinnamon

2 tablespoons soft reduced-fat margarine or
    3 tablespoons soft regular margarine

½ cup chopped almonds, pecans, or
    walnuts

1. Preheat the oven to 375 degrees.
2. Drain the fruits, reserving ½ cup of the juice, and cut into 1-inch pieces. Place 1 tablespoon of the juice in a 2-quart pot, add the cornstarch, and stir to dissolve the cornstarch. Add the sugar substitute, cinnamon, nutmeg, and remaining reserved juice and stir to mix well. Place the pot over medium heat and cook, stirring constantly, for a couple of minutes, or until the mixture is thickened and bubbly. Stir in the drained fruits and set aside.
3. To make the topping, place the oats, wheat germ, brown sugar, and cinnamon in a medium bowl and stir to mix. Add the margarine and stir until the mixture is moist and crumbly. Stir in the nuts.
4. Sprinkle the topping over the fruit and bake uncovered for about 20 minutes, or until the filling is bubbly around the edges and the topping is golden brown. Let sit for 20 minutes before serving.

Nutritional Facts (per serving)
Calories: 159   *Carbohydrates:* 27g   *Cholesterol:* 0mg   *Fat:* 5g   *Sat Fat:* 0.7g
Fiber: 2.7g   *Protein:* 3.4g   *Sodium:* 32mg   *Calcium:* 32mg
   Diabetic exchanges: 2 carbohydrate, 1 fat

Heartwarming Apple Cobbler

YIELD: 8 SERVINGS

1 tablespoon cornstarch

½ cup apple juice

6 cups sliced peeled cooking apples such as
  Fuji, Gala, or Golden Delicious

½ teaspoon ground cinnamon

¼ teaspoon ground nutmeg

Pinch salt

Sugar substitute equal to ½ cup sugar

TOPPING

¾ cup unbleached flour

¼ cup oat bran

¼ cup sugar

¼ teaspoon baking soda

½ cup nonfat or low-fat buttermilk

2 tablespoons canola oil

1. Preheat the oven to 375 degrees.

2. Place the cornstarch and 1 tablespoon of the apple juice in a small bowl and stir to dissolve the cornstarch. Set aside.

3. Place the apples, remaining juice, cinnamon, nutmeg, and salt in a 3-quart pot. Cover and cook over medium heat for about 7 minutes, or just until the apples are tender. Add the sugar substitute and cornstarch mixture and cook for another minute or until thick and bubbly. Set aside to keep warm.

4. While the apple mixture is cooking, place the flour, oat bran, sugar, and baking soda in a medium bowl and stir to mix well. Add the buttermilk and oil and stir to mix well.

5. Coat a shallow 2-quart casserole dish or a 9-inch deep-dish pie pan with cooking spray and spread the apple mixture evenly in the dish. Drop the topping mixture over the hot apple mixture to make 8 biscuits. Bake uncovered for about 15 minutes, or until the biscuits are lightly browned. Let the cobbler sit for 20 minutes before serving. Serve warm.

Nutritional Facts (per serving)

Calories: 169 *Carbohydrates:* 33g *Cholesterol:* 0mg *Fat:* 4g *Sat Fat:* 0.4g
Fiber: 2.3g *Protein:* 2.3g *Sodium:* 73mg *Calcium:* 24mg
  Diabetic exchanges: 2 carbohydrate, 1 fat

Biscuit-topped Blackberry Cobbler

For variety, substitute blueberries or pitted dark sweet cherries for the blackberries.

YIELD: 8 SERVINGS

5 cups fresh or partially thawed
   (undrained) blackberries

1 tablespoon plus 1 teaspoon
   cornstarch

Sugar substitute equal to
   ½ cup sugar

¼ cup orange or white grape juice

TOPPING

¾ cup unbleached flour

¼ cup oat bran

¼ cup sugar

¼ teaspoon baking soda

½ cup nonfat or low-fat buttermilk

2 tablespoons canola oil

1. Preheat the oven to 375 degrees.
2. Place the berries, cornstarch, sugar substitute, and juice in a large bowl and toss to mix well.
3. Coat a shallow 2-quart casserole dish or a 9-inch deep-dish pie pan with cooking spray and spread the berry mixture evenly in the dish. Cover the dish with aluminum foil and bake for about 30 minutes, or until the mixture is hot and bubbly.
4. While the berry mixture is cooking, place the flour, oat bran, sugar, and baking soda in a medium bowl and stir to mix well. Add the buttermilk and oil and stir to mix well.
5. Drop rounded tablespoons of the topping mixture over the hot berry mixture to make 8 biscuits. Bake uncovered for about 15 minutes, or until the biscuits are lightly browned. Let the cobbler sit for 20 minutes before serving warm.

Nutritional Facts (per serving)

Calories: 166   *Carbohydrates:* 32g   *Cholesterol:* 0mg   *Fat:* 4.1g   *Sat Fat:* 0.4g

Fiber: 5.5g   *Protein:* 2.9g   *Sodium:* 56mg   *Calcium:* 49mg

   Diabetic exchanges: 2 carbohydrate, 1 fat

Quick Cherry Cobbler

2 cans (20 ounces each) no-added-sugar or light (reduced-sugar) cherry pie filling

TOPPING
¾ cup unbleached flour
¼ cup oat bran

¼ cup sugar

¼ teaspoon baking soda

½ cup plus 2 tablespoons light vanilla yogurt

2 tablespoons canola oil

1. Preheat the oven to 375 degrees.
2. Coat a shallow 2-quart casserole dish or a 9-inch deep-dish pie pan with cooking spray and spread the pie filling evenly in the dish. Cover the dish with aluminum foil and bake for about 25 minutes, or until the pie filling is hot and bubbly.
3. While the filling is heating, place the flour, oat bran, sugar, and baking soda in a medium bowl and stir to mix well. Add the yogurt and oil and stir to mix well.
4. Drop the topping mixture over the hot cherry filling to make 8 biscuits. Bake uncovered for about 15 minutes, or until the biscuits are lightly browned. Let the cobbler sit for 20 minutes before serving. Serve warm.

Nutritional Facts (per serving)
Calories: 169 *Carbohydrates:* 31g *Cholesterol:* 0mg *Fat:* 3.6g *Sat Fat:* 0.3g
Fiber: 1.5g *Protein:* 2.5g *Sodium:* 77mg *Calcium:* 33mg
Diabetic exchanges: 2 carbohydrate, 1 fat

Ginger-Baked Peaches

YIELD: 4 SERVINGS

2 large fresh peaches (8 ounces each)

2 tablespoons white grape juice

TOPPING

½ cup finely crushed gingersnaps

¼ cup sliced almonds or chopped pecans

1 tablespoon plus 1 teaspoon melted margarine or butter

1 tablespoon plus 1 teaspoon frozen white grape juice concentrate, thawed

1. Cut the peaches in half lengthwise and remove the pits. Cut a thin slice off the bottom of each peach half so it will sit upright. Place the peach halves in an 8-inch square pan and pour the juice into the bottom of the pan. Set aside.
2. To make the topping, place the gingersnaps and nuts in a small bowl. Add the margarine and juice concentrate and stir until moist and crumbly. Mound a quarter of the mixture into the center of each peach half.
3. Bake uncovered at 375 degrees for about 20 minutes, or until the peaches are tender and the topping is golden brown. Cover the peaches loosely with foil during the last part of baking if the topping starts to brown too quickly. Serve warm, plain or with a scoop of light vanilla ice cream if desired.

Nutritional Facts (per serving)

Calories: 181   *Carbohydrates:* 26g   *Cholesterol:* 0mg   *Fat:* 7.8g   *Sat Fat:* 1.5g

Fiber: 3g   *Protein:* 3g   *Sodium:* 125mg   *Calcium:* 31mg

Diabetic exchanges: 2 carbohydrate, 1½ fat

Pears with Cinnamon Crunch Stuffing

YIELD: 4 SERVINGS

2 large pears (8 ounces each)

3 tablespoons orange or apple juice

2 tablespoons light brown sugar

¼ teaspoon ground cinnamon

2 teaspoons maple syrup

2 teaspoons soft margarine

TOPPING

¼ cup chopped walnuts

¼ cup quick-cooking (1-minute) oats

1. Cut the pears in half lengthwise and use a spoon to scoop out the seeds, creating a small depression. Cut a thin slice off the bottom of each pear half so it will sit upright. Place the pear halves in an 8-inch square pan and pour the juice into the bottom of the pan. Set aside.

2. To make the topping, place the walnuts, oats, brown sugar, and cinnamon in a small bowl and stir to mix. Add the maple syrup and margarine and stir to mix. Mound a quarter of the mixture into the center of each pear half.

3. Bake uncovered at 375 degrees for about 20 minutes, or until the pears are tender and the topping is golden brown. Cover the pears loosely with foil during the last part of baking if the topping starts to brown too quickly. Serve warm, plain or with a scoop of light vanilla ice cream if desired.

Nutritional Facts (per serving)

Calories: 181   *Carbohydrates:* 30g   *Cholesterol:* 0mg   *Fat:* 6.7g   *Sat Fat:* 0.8g

Fiber: 0.5g   *Protein:* 3.2g   *Sodium:* 18mg   *Calcium:* 28mg

Diabetic exchanges: 2 carbohydrate, 1 fat

Honey-Roasted Plums

YIELD: 6 SERVINGS

6 large firm but ripe plums, halved
   and pitted

¾ cup orange juice

3 tablespoons honey

1 ½ tablespoons melted margarine
   or butter

¼ teaspoon ground cinnamon

1. Preheat the oven to 425 degrees.
2. Coat a 9-by-13-inch pan with nonstick cooking spray and arrange the plums, cut side down, in a single layer in the pan. Combine the orange juice, honey, margarine or butter, and cinnamon and stir to mix well. Pour the orange juice mixture over the plums.
3. Bake uncovered for 12 minutes, turn the plums over, and bake for an additional 12 minutes, basting occasionally with the pan juices, or until the plums are tender.
4. Remove the dish from the oven and let sit for 10 minutes before serving warm.

Nutritional Facts (per serving)
Calories: 116   *Carbohydrates:* 24g   *Cholesterol:* 0mg   *Fat:* 2.9g   *Sat Fat:* 0.6g
Fiber: 1.3g   *Protein:* 1g   *Sodium:* 23mg   *Calcium:* 4mg   *Iron:* 0.1mg
   Diabetic exchanges: 1½ carbohydrate, ½ fat

Bananas with Rum Sauce

YIELD: 4 SERVINGS

SAUCE

½ teaspoon cornstarch

¼ cup orange juice

2 tablespoons rum

1 tablespoon plus 1 teaspoon brown sugar

Sugar substitute equal to ¼ cup sugar

BANANAS

1 tablespoon plus 1 teaspoon margarine
  or butter

2 large peeled bananas, halved crosswise
  and then lengthwise

2 to 3 tablespoons chopped pecans

1. To make the sauce, place the cornstarch in a small bowl, add a teaspoon of the juice and stir to dissolve the cornstarch. Stir in the remaining juice and then the rum, brown sugar, and sugar substitute. Set aside.

2. Place the margarine or butter in a large nonstick skillet and melt over medium heat. Add the bananas and cook for about a minute on each side, or until heated through. (Do not overcook.)

3. Pour the sauce over the bananas and cook and stir for a minute, until the sauce is thickened and bubbly. Divide the mixture between 4 dessert plates and top each serving with a sprinkling of the pecans. Serve hot.

Nutritional Facts (per serving)
Calories: 162   *Carbohydrate:* 24g   *Cholesterol:* 0mg   *Fat:* 6g   *Sat Fat:* 1.2g
Fiber: 2g   *Protein:* 1.2g   *Sodium:* 33mg   *Calcium:* 12mg
Diabetic exchanges: 1½ carbohydrate, 1 fat

Broiled Peaches with Cinnamon & Brown Sugar

YIELD: 4 SERVINGS

2 large peaches (8 ounces each)

2 ½ tablespoons light brown sugar

½ teaspoon ground cinnamon

1. Cut the peaches in half and remove the pits. Cut a thin slice off the bottom of each peach half so it will sit upright. Place the peach halves, cut side up, on a small baking sheet. Broil for about 3 minutes, or until the peaches start to soften.
2. Combine the cinnamon and sugar and sprinkle a quarter of the mixture over each peach half. Broil for another minute, or until the sugar is melted and bubbly. Serve warm.

Nutritional Facts (per serving)
Calories: 81   *Carbohydrates:* 21g   *Cholesterol:* 0mg   *Fat:* 0.1g   *Sat Fat:* 0g
Fiber: 2.3g   *Protein:* 0.8g   *Sodium:* 3mg   *Calcium:* 13mg
Diabetic exchanges: 1½ carbohydrate

Spiced Apples

YIELD: 4 SERVINGS

4 cups sliced peeled cooking apples such as Gala, Fuji, or Golden Delicious
¼ cup plus 2 tablespoons apple juice
1 teaspoon cornstarch

¼ teaspoon ground cinnamon
¼ teaspoon ground nutmeg
Sugar substitute equal to ¼ cup sugar

1. Place the apples and ¼ cup of the juice in a 2-quart nonstick pot and place over medium heat. Cover and cook, stirring occasionally, for about 5 minutes, or just until the apples are tender.
2. Combine the cornstarch, cinnamon, nutmeg, and sugar substitute and stir to mix. Add the remaining apple juice and stir until the cornstarch is completely dissolved. Pour the cornstarch mixture over the apples and cook for another minute, or until the mixture thickens slightly. Serve hot.

Nutritional Facts (per ½-cup serving)
Calories: 75   *Carbohydrates:* 19g   *Cholesterol:* 0mg   *Fat:* 0.4g   *Sat Fat:* 0.1g
Fiber: 2g   *Protein:* 0.2g   *Sodium:* 1mg   *Calcium:* 9mg
Diabetic exchanges: 1 carbohydrate

Strawberries with Chocolate and Almonds

YIELD: 30 PIECES

30 medium strawberries (about 1 pound)

1 cup sliced almonds, crushed

8 ounces chopped dark or semisweet chocolate (about 1⅓ cups)

1. Rinse the berries with cool water (leave the stems on) and pat dry thoroughly with paper towels. Set aside.
2. Place the almonds in a shallow dish and set aside.
3. Fill a 2-quart pot ⅓ full with water and bring to a boil. Reduce the heat to low to keep the water barely simmering. While the water is heating up, place the chocolate in a 2-cup glass measure and microwave at high power for a couple of minutes, stirring twice, until the chocolate is melted and smooth. Place the measuring cup in the pot of simmering water to keep the chocolate liquefied.
4. Dip a berry in the melted chocolate to coat the lower three-quarters of the berry. Then roll the chocolate-coated berry in the almonds. Cover a large baking sheet with waxed paper and place the berry on the sheet. Coat the remaining berries in the same manner and then place the baking sheet in the refrigerator for 30 minutes to allow the chocolate to harden. Serve immediately or cover and refrigerate for up to 12 hours before serving.

Nutritional Facts (per berry)

Calories: 54   Carbohydrates: 5g   Cholesterol: 0mg   Fat: 4.3g   Sat Fat: 1.8g
Fiber: 0.8g   Protein: 1.2g   Sodium: 1mg   Calcium: 12mg

Diabetic exchanges: ⅓ carbohydrate, 1 fat

Berries with Honey-Lime Cream

½ cup light sour cream

2 tablespoons honey

Sugar substitute equal to 1 to 2 tablespoons
    sugar

2 teaspoons lime juice

¾ cups sliced strawberries

¾ cup fresh blueberries or blackberries

¾ cup fresh raspberries

2 tablespoons sliced almonds

1. Combine the sour cream, honey, sugar substitute, and lime juice in a small bowl and stir to mix well. Combine the berries in a bowl and toss to mix.
2. To serve, place a quarter of the berries in each of four 8-ounce dessert dishes. Top each serving with a quarter of the sour-cream mixture and a sprinkling of almonds. Serve immediately.

Nutritional Facts (per serving)
Calories: 122   *Carbohydrates:* 18g   *Cholesterol:* 10mg   *Fat:* 4.5g   *Sat Fat:* 2g
Fiber: 3.3g   *Protein:* 3.3g   *Sodium:* 27mg   *Calcium:* 58mg
    Diabetic exchanges: 1 carbohydrate

Spiked Summer Fruits

2 cups sliced peeled fresh peaches (about
    3 medium)

1 cup sliced fresh unpeeled plums (about
    3 medium)

½ cup fresh blueberries, rinsed and
    patted dry

½ cup fresh raspberries, rinsed and
    patted dry

1½ tablespoons honey

1½ tablespoons apricot brandy

4 fresh mint sprigs (optional)

1. Place the fruits in a shallow bowl. Combine the honey and brandy in a small bowl and stir to mix. Pour the honey mixture over the fruits and toss gently to mix.

2. Let the mixture sit at room temperature for 20 to 30 minutes to allow the flavors to blend. Divide the mixture between 5 dessert dishes, garnish with a mint sprig if desired, and serve immediately.

> **Nutritional Facts (per serving)**
> *Calories:* 94   *Carbohydrates:* 22g   *Cholesterol:* 0mg   *Fat:* 0.4g   *Sat Fat:* 0g
> *Fiber:* 3.1g   *Protein:* 1g   *Sodium:* 1mg   *Calcium:* 9mg
> **Diabetic exchanges:** 1½ carbohydrate

Refreshing Fruit Cup

YIELD: 5 SERVINGS

2 cups sliced fresh strawberries

1½ cups diced fresh mango

¾ cup fresh blueberries

Sugar substitute equal to 1 tablespoon sugar

2 tablespoons honey

2 teaspoons lime juice

3 tablespoons sliced almonds

1. Place the fruits and sugar substitute in a medium bowl and toss to mix well. Divide the mixture between five 8-ounce dessert dishes.

2. Place the honey and lime juice in a small bowl and stir to mix well. Drizzle some of the mixture over each dish of fruit. Serve immediately, topping each serving with a sprinkling of the almonds.

> **Nutritional Facts (per serving)**
> *Calories:* 111   *Carbohydrates:* 24g   *Cholesterol:* 0mg   *Fat:* 2.4g   *Sat Fat:* 0.2g
> *Fiber:* 3.5g   *Protein:* 1.7g   *Sodium:* 3mg   *Calcium:* 25mg
> **Diabetic exchanges:** 1½ carbohydrate, ½ fat

8. Delightful Dessert Breads

Quick breads and other sweet breads are among the most versatile of desserts. Spread with light cream cheese or served with a glass of low-fat milk, they can double as a light breakfast or between-meals snack. Filled with fruits and nuts and topped with a drizzle of sweet glaze or a crumb topping, dessert breads can also make a show-stopping addition to an elegant brunch or afternoon tea.

Like most baked goods, dessert breads require some sugar if they are to have a moist and tender texture and nicely browned crust. However, most sweet breads can be made with about half the usual amount of sugar. As you will see, wholesome ingredients like oat flour and whole-wheat pastry flour, naturally sweet fruits, and a dash of cinnamon, nutmeg, and other sweet spices allow you to use a relatively small amount of sweetener and still enjoy luscious results.

Whether you are looking for a festive fruit-and-nut loaf for holiday gift giving, a warm fruit-filled yeast bread to serve with coffee or tea, or a whole-wheat banana-nut bread to go with a glass of cold milk, you need look no further. This chapter presents a variety of sweet and delightful loaves that are sure to be requested time and time again.

Apple-Nut Bread

YIELD: 16 SLICES

1½ cups whole-wheat pastry flour

1 teaspoon ground cinnamon

¼ teaspoon ground nutmeg

½ teaspoon baking powder

½ teaspoon baking soda

¼ teaspoon salt

½ cup brown sugar

Sugar substitute equal to ½ cup sugar

¼ cup canola oil

¼ cup fat-free egg substitute

1 cup peeled shredded apple (about 3 medium)

3 tablespoons apple juice

½ cup chopped walnuts or toasted pecans (page 25)

1. Preheat the oven to 350 degrees.

2. Place the flour, cinnamon, nutmeg, baking powder, baking soda, and salt in a medium bowl and stir to mix well. Add the brown sugar and sugar substitute and stir to mix well. Use the back of a wooden spoon to press out the lumps in the brown sugar.

3. Add the oil, egg substitute, apple, and apple juice to the flour mixture and stir to mix. Fold in the nuts.

4. Coat the bottom only of an 8-by-4-inch pan with cooking spray and spread the batter evenly in the pan. Bake for 40 to 45 minutes, or just until a wooden toothpick inserted in the center of the loaf comes out clean. Let the cake cool in the pan for 10 minutes then turn onto a wire rack and cool to room temperature. Wrap and store overnight before slicing and serving.

Nutritional Facts (per slice)

Calories: 130   *Carbohydrates:* 18g   *Cholesterol:* 0mg   *Fat:* 5.8g   *Sat Fat:* 0.4g
Fiber: 2g   *Protein:* 2.8g   *Sodium:* 94mg   *Calcium:* 10mg

  Diabetic exchanges: 1 carbohydrate, 1 fat

Zucchini-Spice Bread

1½ cups whole-wheat pastry flour

1 teaspoon ground cinnamon

½ teaspoon ground nutmeg

½ teaspoon dried lemon rind

½ teaspoon baking powder

½ teaspoon baking soda

¼ teaspoon salt

½ cup light brown sugar

Sugar substitute equal to ½ cup sugar

¼ cup canola oil

¼ cup fat-free egg substitute

1 cup shredded zucchini (about 1 medium)

2 tablespoons nonfat or low-fat milk

½ cup chopped walnuts (page 25)

1. Preheat the oven to 350 degrees.
2. Place the flour, cinnamon, nutmeg, lemon rind, baking powder, baking soda, and salt in a medium bowl and stir to mix well. Add the brown sugar and sugar substitute and stir to mix well. Use the back of a wooden spoon to press out the lumps in the brown sugar.
3. Add the oil, egg substitute, zucchini, and milk to the flour mixture and stir to mix. Fold in the nuts.
4. Coat the bottom only of an 8-by-4-inch pan with cooking spray and spread the batter evenly in the pan. Bake for 40 to 45 minutes, or just until a wooden toothpick inserted in the center of the loaf comes out clean. Let the cake cool in the pan for 10 minutes then turn onto a wire rack and cool to room temperature. Wrap and store overnight before slicing and serving.

Nutritional Facts (per slice)
Calories: 128   *Carbohydrates:* 17g   *Cholesterol:* 0mg   *Fat:* 5.8g   *Sat Fat:* 0.4g
Fiber: 2g   *Protein:* 3g   *Sodium:* 95mg   *Calcium:* 14mg
   Diabetic exchanges: 1 carbohydrate, 1 fat

Whole-Wheat Banana-Nut Bread

YIELD: 16 SLICES

1½ cups whole-wheat pastry flour

½ cup sugar

Sugar substitute equal to ⅓ cup sugar

1 teaspoon baking powder

½ teaspoon baking soda

½ teaspoon ground cardamom or
   nutmeg

¼ teaspoon salt

1 cup mashed very ripe banana
   (about 2 large)

¼ cup canola oil

¼ cup fat-free egg substitute

½ cup chopped walnuts or toasted pecans
   (page 25)

1. Preheat the oven to 350 degrees.
2. Place the flour, sugar, sugar substitute, baking powder, baking soda, cardamom or nutmeg, and salt in a medium bowl and stir to mix well
3. Add the banana, oil, and egg substitute to the flour mixture and stir to mix. Fold in the nuts.
4. Coat the bottom only of an 8-by-4-inch pan with cooking spray and spread the batter evenly in the pan. Bake at 350 degrees for 40 to 45 minutes, or just until a wooden toothpick inserted in the center of the loaf comes out clean. Let the cake cool in the pan for 15 minutes, then turn onto a wire rack and cool to room temperature. Wrap and store overnight before slicing and serving.

Nutritional Facts (per slice)
Calories: 135   *Carbohydrates:* 19g   *Cholesterol:* 0mg   *Fat:* 5.8g   *Sat Fat:* 0.4g
Fiber: 2g   *Protein:* 3g   *Sodium:* 98mg   *Calcium:* 4mg
   Diabetic exchanges: 1 carbohydrate, 1 fat

Cocoa Banana Bread

1 cup plus 2 tablespoons whole-wheat pastry flour

¼ cup plus 2 tablespoons Dutch-processed cocoa powder

¾ teaspoon baking soda

¼ teaspoon salt

½ cup light brown sugar

Sugar substitute equal to ½ cup sugar

1 cup mashed very ripe banana (about 2 large)

¼ cup canola oil

¼ cup fat-free egg substitute

1 teaspoon vanilla extract

½ cup chopped walnuts or toasted pecans (page 25)

1. Preheat the oven to 350 degrees.
2. Place the flour, cocoa, baking soda, and salt in a medium bowl and stir to mix well. Add the brown sugar and sugar substitute and stir to mix. Use the back of a spoon to press out any lumps in the brown sugar.
3. Add the banana, oil, egg substitute, and vanilla extract to the flour mixture and stir to mix. Fold in the nuts.
4. Coat the bottom only of an 8-by-4-inch pan with cooking spray and spread the batter evenly in the pan. Bake at 350 degrees for about 40 minutes, or just until a wooden toothpick inserted in the center of the loaf comes out clean. Let the cake cool in the pan for 10 minutes, then turn onto a wire rack and cool to room temperature. Wrap and store overnight before slicing and serving.

Nutritional Facts (per slice)

Calories: 134 *Carbohydrates:* 19g *Cholesterol:* 0mg *Fat:* 6g *Sat Fat:* 0.5g
Fiber: 2.3g *Protein:* 3.2g *Sodium:* 74mg *Calcium:* 33mg
   Diabetic exchanges: 1 carbohydrate, 1 fat

Cranberry-Pecan Bread

YIELD: 16 SLICES

1 cup whole-wheat pastry flour

¾ cup oat flour

½ cup sugar

Sugar substitute equal to ½ cup sugar

1 teaspoon dried orange rind

1 teaspoon baking powder

½ teaspoon baking soda

¼ teaspoon salt

⅔ cup orange juice

3 tablespoons canola oil

¼ cup fat-free egg substitute

1 cup coarsely chopped fresh or frozen cranberries

½ cup chopped toasted pecans (page 25)

1. Preheat the oven to 350 degrees.
2. Place the flours, sugar, sugar substitute, orange rind, baking powder, baking soda, and salt in a medium bowl and stir to mix well.
3. Add the orange juice, oil, and egg substitute to the flour mixture and stir to mix well. Set the batter aside for 10 minutes. Stir the batter several times and then fold in the cranberries and pecans.
4. Coat the bottom only of an 8-by-4-inch pan with cooking spray and spread the batter evenly in the pan. Bake for 40 to 45 minutes, or just until a wooden toothpick inserted in the center of the loaf comes out clean. Let the cake cool in the pan for 15 minutes, then turn onto a wire rack and cool to room temperature. Wrap and store overnight before slicing and serving.

Nutritional Facts (per slice)

Calories: 127   Carbohydrates: 18g   Cholesterol: 0mg   Fat: 5.7g   Sat Fat: 0.4g
Fiber: 2.2g   Protein: 2.5g   Sodium: 114mg   Calcium: 25mg
   Diabetic exchanges: 1 carbohydrate, 1 fat

Pumpkin-Pecan Bread

YIELD: 16 SLICES

1½ cups whole-wheat pastry flour

2 teaspoons baking powder

¼ teaspoon baking soda

1 teaspoon pumpkin pie spice

Scant ¼ teaspoon salt

½ cup light brown sugar

Sugar substitute equal to ½ cup sugar

¾ cup canned or cooked mashed pumpkin

¼ cup plus 2 tablespoons nonfat or
   low-fat milk

¼ cup fat-free egg substitute

¼ cup canola oil

½ cup chopped toasted pecans
   (page 25)

⅓ cup finely chopped golden raisins or dried
   cranberries (optional)

1. Preheat the oven to 350 degrees.
2. Place the flour, baking powder, baking soda, pie spice, and salt in a medium bowl and stir to mix well. Add the brown sugar and sugar substitute and stir to mix well. Use the back of a wooden spoon to press out the lumps in the brown sugar.
3. Combine the pumpkin, milk, egg substitute, and oil in a bowl and stir to mix well. Add the pumpkin mixture to the flour mixture and stir to mix well. Add the nuts and the raisins or dried cranberries, if using.
4. Coat the bottom only of an 8-by-4-inch pan with cooking spray and spread the batter evenly in the pan. Bake for about 40 minutes, or just until a wooden toothpick inserted in the center of the loaf comes out clean. Let the cake cool in the pan for 10 minutes then turn onto a wire rack and cool to room temperature. Wrap and store overnight before slicing and serving.

Nutritional Facts (per slice)

Calories: 132   Carbohydrates: 18g   Cholesterol: 0mg   Fat: 6.3g   Sat Fat: 0.5g
Fiber: 2.2g   Protein: 2.6g   Sodium: 125mg   Calcium: 57mg
   Diabetic exchanges: 1 carbohydrate, 1 fat

Very Blueberry Bread

YIELD: 16 SLICES

¾ cup whole-wheat pastry flour

¾ cup oat flour

½ cup sugar

Sugar substitute equal to ½ cup sugar

½ teaspoon dried lemon rind

1 teaspoon baking powder

¼ teaspoon baking soda

⅔ cup nonfat or low-fat buttermilk

¼ cup fat-free egg substitute

¼ cup canola oil

⅓ cup chopped walnuts (optional)

¾ cup fresh or frozen (unthawed) blueberries

1. Preheat the oven to 350 degrees.
2. Place the flours, sugar, sugar substitute, lemon rind, baking powder, and baking soda, in a medium bowl and stir to mix well.
3. Combine the buttermilk, egg substitute, and oil in a small bowl and stir to mix. Add the buttermilk mixture to the flour mixture and stir to mix well. Set the batter aside for 10 minutes. Stir for 10 seconds and then fold in the nuts, if using.
4. Coat the bottom only of an 8-by-4-inch pan with cooking spray and spread ⅓ of the batter evenly in the pan, scatter a scant ⅓ cup of the berries over the batter. Repeat the batter and berry layers and finish off with the remaining batter and berries.
5. Bake for 40 to 45 minutes, or just until a wooden toothpick inserted in the center of the loaf comes out clean. Let the cake cool in the pan for 10 minutes then turn onto a wire rack and cool to room temperature. Wrap and store overnight before slicing and serving.

Nutritional Facts (per slice)
Calories: 105   *Carbohydrates:* 16g   *Cholesterol:* 0mg   *Fat:* 3.9g   *Sat Fat:* 0.3g
Fiber: 1.5g   *Protein:* 2.3g   *Sodium:* 70mg   *Calcium:* 35mg
Diabetic exchanges: 1 carbohydrate, 1 fat

Carrot-Raisin Bread

1 cup whole-wheat pastry flour

½ cup oat flour

1 teaspoon ground cinnamon

¼ teaspoon ground nutmeg

½ teaspoon baking powder

½ teaspoon baking soda

½ cup light brown sugar

Sugar substitute equal to ½ cup sugar

1¼ cups (moderately packed) grated carrots

½ cup plus 2 tablespoons nonfat or low-fat milk

¼ cup canola oil

¼ cup fat-free egg substitute

⅓ cup dark or golden raisins

⅓ cup chopped walnuts

1. Preheat the oven to 350 degrees.
2. Place the flours, cinnamon, nutmeg, baking powder, and baking soda in a medium bowl and stir to mix well. Add the brown sugar and sugar substitute and stir to mix well. Use the back of a wooden spoon to press out the lumps in the brown sugar.
3. Add the carrots, milk, oil, and egg substitute to the flour mixture and stir to mix. Fold in the raisins and nuts.
4. Coat the bottom only of an 8-by-4-inch pan with cooking spray and spread the batter evenly in the pan. Bake for about 45 minutes, or just until a wooden toothpick inserted in the center of the loaf comes out clean. Let the cake cool in the pan for 10 minutes then turn onto a wire rack and cool to room temperature. Wrap and store overnight before slicing and serving.

Nutritional Facts (per slice)

Calories: 128 *Carbohydrates:* 19g *Cholesterol:* 0mg *Fat:* 5.2g *Sat Fat:* 0.4g
Fiber: 2g *Protein:* 3g *Sodium:* 69mg *Calcium:* 23mg
Diabetic exchanges: 1 carbohydrate, 1 fat

Whole-Wheat Sweet Dough

YIELD: ABOUT ¾ POUND, OR 12 SERVINGS

1⅓ cups unbleached flour

⅔ cup whole-wheat pastry flour

3 tablespoons sugar

Sugar substitute equal to 3 tablespoons sugar

1 packet (¼ ounce) rapid rise yeast (about
2 teaspoons)

¼ teaspoon salt

¼ cup plus 2 tablespoons nonfat or
low-fat milk

¼ cup fat-free egg substitute

2 tablespoons margarine or butter

1. Place all of the ingredients except for 2 tablespoons of the unbleached flour in the pan of a bread machine. Turn the machine to the "rise," "dough," "manual," or equivalent setting so the machine will mix, knead, and let the dough rise once.

2. Check the dough about 3 minutes after the machine has started. If the dough seems too sticky, add more of the remaining flour, a tablespoon at a time. When the dough is ready, remove it from the machine and proceed to shape, fill, and bake it as directed in the recipe of your choice.

Nutritional Facts (per serving)

Calories: 99   *Carbohydrates:* 18g   *Cholesterol:* 0mg   *Fat:* 1.6g   *Sat Fat:* 0.4g

Fiber: 1.2g   *Protein:* 3g   *Sodium:* 78mg   *Calcium:* 11mg

Diabetic exchanges: 1 carbohydrate, ½ fat

Variation: Hand-Mixing Method

If you don't own a bread machine, you can make this dough using the following steps:

1. Combine all of the whole-wheat flour, sugar, sugar substitute, yeast, and salt, and stir to mix well.

2. Heat the milk and margarine or butter until very warm (130 degrees) and gradu-

ally stir into the flour mixture. Stir for 1 minute and then stir in the egg substitute. Stir in the unbleached flour, 2 tablespoons at a time, until the dough is too stiff to continue mixing by hand.

3. Turn the dough onto a floured surface and knead the dough for 5 minutes, gradually incorporating enough of the remaining unbleached flour to form a smooth, satiny ball.

4. Coat a large bowl with cooking spray and place the dough in the bowl. Cover the bowl with a clean kitchen towel and let rise in a warm place for about 1 hour, or until doubled in size. Then proceed to shape, fill, and bake the dough according to recipe directions.

·: *Braided Apple Bread* :·

YIELD: 12 SERVINGS

1 recipe Whole-Wheat Sweet Dough
   (page 168)

1 teaspoon nonfat or low-fat milk

1/8 teaspoon ground nutmeg

1/4 cup dark raisins

FILLING

1 1/2 cups no-added-sugar or light
   (reduced-sugar) apple pie filling,
   chopped

1/4 teaspoon ground cinnamon

GLAZE

1/4 cup powdered sugar

1 teaspoon nonfat or low-fat milk

1/8 teaspoon vanilla extract

Pinch ground cinnamon

2 tablespoons finely chopped walnuts

1. To make the filling, place pie filling, cinnamon, and nutmeg in a small bowl and stir to mix. Stir in the raisins and set aside.

2. Place the dough on a lightly floured surface and roll it into a 10-by-12-inch rectangle. Coat a large baking sheet with cooking spray and transfer the dough to the sheet.

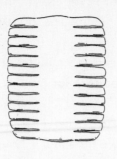

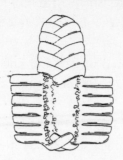

a. Make 3¼-inch-long cuts at 1-inch intervals on each side of the dough.

b. Fold the dough strips diagonally over the filling.

c. Continue folding the strips to create a "braided" loaf.

Making Braided Apple Bread, Cherry-Cheese Loaf, and Peach Streusel Bread

3. Using a sharp knife, make 3 ¼-inch-long cuts at 1-inch intervals on both of the 12-inch sides. Spread the apple filling down the center of the dough. Fold the strips diagonally over the filling, overlapping them to create a braided look. (See the figures shown above for clarification). Cover the loaf with a clean kitchen towel and let it rise in a warm place for about 45 minutes, or until doubled in size.

4. Lightly brush the top of the loaf with the milk. Bake at 350 degrees for about 20 minutes, or until the loaf is lightly browned and no longer doughy in the center. Cover loosely with aluminum foil during the last part of baking if the loaf begins to brown too quickly.

5. To make the glaze, combine all of the glaze ingredients except the nuts in a small bowl and stir until smooth. Drizzle the glaze over the warm loaf and sprinkle with the walnuts. Serve warm.

Nutritional Facts (per slice)
Calories: 136   *Carbohydrates:* 26g   *Cholesterol:* 0mg   *Fat:* 2.3g   *Sat Fat:* 0.5g
Fiber: 1.8g   *Protein:* 3.4g   *Sodium:* 86mg   *Calcium:* 13 mg
    Diabetic exchanges: 2 carbohydrate, ½ fat

Cherry-Cheese Loaf

YIELD: 12 SERVINGS

1 recipe Whole-Wheat Sweet Dough
   (page 168)

1 teaspoon nonfat or low-fat milk

Sugar substitute equal to ¼ cup sugar

¾ cup no-added-sugar or light (reduced-sugar) cherry pie filling

FILLING

6 ounces nonfat or reduced-fat cream cheese

1½ tablespoons fat-free egg substitute

1½ teaspoons unbleached flour

½ teaspoon vanilla extract

GLAZE

¼ cup powdered sugar

1 teaspoon nonfat or low-fat milk

⅛ teaspoon vanilla extract

2 tablespoons sliced almonds

1. To make the filling, place the cream cheese, egg substitute, flour, vanilla, and sugar substitute in a small bowl and beat with an electric mixer until smooth. Set aside.

2. Place the dough on a lightly floured surface and roll it into a 10-by-12-inch rectangle. Coat a large baking sheet with cooking spray and transfer the dough to the sheet.

3. Using a sharp knife, make 3 ¼-inch-long cuts at 1-inch intervals on both of the 12-inch sides. Spread the cheese filling down the center of the dough, then cover the cheese filling with the cherry pie filling. Fold the strips diagonally over the filling, overlapping them to create a braided look. (See the figures on page 170 for clarification). Cover the loaf with a clean kitchen towel and let it rise in a warm place for about 45 minutes, or until doubled in size.

4. Lightly brush the top of the loaf with the milk. Bake at 350 degrees for about 20 minutes, or until the loaf is lightly browned and no longer doughy in the center. Cover loosely with aluminum foil during the last part of baking if the loaf begins to brown too quickly.

5. To make the glaze, combine all of the glaze ingredients except the almonds in a small bowl and stir until smooth. Drizzle the glaze over the warm loaf and sprinkle with the almonds. Serve warm.

Nutritional Facts (per slice)

Calories: 137   *Carbohydrates:* 23g   *Cholesterol:* 1mg   *Fat:* 2.1g   *Sat Fat:* 0.5g

Fiber: 1.4g   *Protein:* 5.6g   *Sodium:* 153mg   *Calcium:* 57mg

Diabetic exchanges: 1½ carbohydrate, ½ fat

∴ Peach Streusel Bread ∴

For variety, substitute canned apricots for the peaches.

YIELD: 12 SERVINGS

1 recipe Whole-Wheat Sweet Dough
  (page 168)

1 teaspoon nonfat or low-fat milk

FILLING

1 tablespoon cornstarch

15-ounce can peaches in juice, drained and
  diced (reserve the juice)

Sugar substitute equal to ¼ cup sugar

TOPPING

1½ tablespoons whole-wheat pastry flour

1½ tablespoons light brown sugar

1½ teaspoons reduced-fat margarine
  or light butter, brought to room
  temperature

3 tablespoons chopped almonds, pecans,
  or walnuts

1. To make the filling, place the cornstarch and 1 tablespoon of the reserved juice in a small bowl, stir to dissolve the cornstarch, and set aside. Place the drained peaches and 3 tablespoons of the reserved juice in a small pot. Bring the peaches to a boil over medium heat. Stir in the sugar substitute and the cornstarch mixture and cook, stirring constantly, for about a minute, or until thickened and bubbly. Set aside to cool.

2. Place the dough on a lightly floured surface and roll it into a 10-by-12-inch rectangle. Coat a large baking sheet with cooking spray and transfer the dough to the sheet.

3. Using a sharp knife, make 3 ¼-inch-long cuts at 1-inch intervals on both of the 12-inch sides. Spread the peach filling down the center of the dough. Fold the

strips diagonally over the filling, overlapping them to create a braided look. (See the figures on page 170 for clarification.) Cover the loaf with a clean kitchen towel and let it rise in a warm place for about 45 minutes, or until doubled in size.

4. To make the topping, place all of the topping ingredients in a small bowl and stir until the mixture is moist and crumbly. Lightly brush the top of the loaf with the milk and sprinkle with the topping.

5. Bake at 350 degrees for about 20 minutes, or until the loaf is lightly browned and no longer doughy in the center. Cover loosely with aluminum foil during the last part of baking if the loaf begins to brown too quickly. Serve warm.

Nutritional Facts (per slice)
Calories: 137   *Carbohydrates:* 25g   *Cholesterol:* 0mg   *Fat:* 2.8g   *Sat Fat:* 0.6g
Fiber: 1.8g   *Protein:* 3.7g   *Sodium:* 84mg   *Calcium:* 19mg
   Diabetic exchanges: 1½ carbohydrate, ½ fat

Blueberry Tea Ring

For variety, substitute chopped pitted cherries or diced strawberries for the blueberries.

YIELD: 12 SERVINGS

1 recipe Whole-Wheat Sweet Dough
   (page 168)

1 teaspoon nonfat or low-fat milk

FILLING
2 cups fresh or frozen blueberries

2 tablespoons orange or white grape juice

Sugar substitute equal to 2 to 3 tablespoons
   sugar

GLAZE
¼ cup powdered sugar

1 teaspoon nonfat or low-fat milk

⅛ teaspoon vanilla extract

2 tablespoons sliced almonds

1. To prepare the filling, place the blueberries and juice in a 2-quart pot and place over medium heat. Cover and cook for several minutes, or until the berries soften and release their juices. Cook uncovered, stirring frequently, for about 5 minutes more, or until the mixture reduces to about ⅔ cup. Stir in the sugar substitute and set aside to cool to room temperature.

2. Place the dough on a lightly floured surface and roll it into a 10-by-12-inch rectangle. Spread the filling over the dough and roll the dough up jelly-roll style, beginning at the long end.

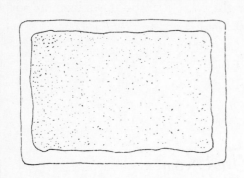

a. Spread the filling over the dough.

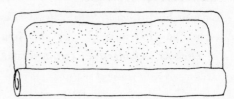

b. Roll the dough up jelly-roll style.

c. Bend the roll into a ring, and cut almost all the way through at 1-inch intervals.

d. Twist each 1-inch segment to turn the the cut side up.

Making Blueberry Tea Ring and Raspberry Tea Ring

3. Coat a large baking sheet with cooking spray and place the roll on the pan, bringing the ends around to form a circle. Using scissors, cut almost all of the way through the dough at 1-inch intervals. Twist each 1-inch segment to turn the cut-side up. (See the figures on page 174 for clarification.) Cover with a clean kitchen towel and let rise in a warm place for about 45 minutes, or until doubled in size.

4. Lightly brush the top of the ring with the milk. Bake at 350 degrees for about 15 minutes, or until lightly browned and no longer doughy in the center. Cover loosely with aluminum foil during the last part of baking if the rings starts to brown too quickly.

5. To make the glaze, combine all of the glaze ingredients except the almonds in a small bowl and stir until smooth. Drizzle the glaze over the warm loaf and sprinkle with the almonds. Serve warm.

Nutritional Facts (per slice)

Calories: 131   *Carbohydrates:* 25g   *Cholesterol:* 0mg   *Fat:* 2.3g   *Sat Fat:* 0.5g

Fiber: 2g   *Protein:* 3.4g   *Sodium:* 79mg   *Calcium:* 15mg

   Diabetic exchanges: 1½ carbohydrate, ½ fat

Raspberry Tea Ring

YIELD: 12 SERVINGS

1 recipe Whole-Wheat Sweet Dough (page 168)

1 teaspoon nonfat or low-fat milk

FILLING

1⅓ cups fresh or frozen raspberries

¼ cup white grape juice

1 tablespoon cornstarch

Sugar substitute equal to ¼ cup sugar

GLAZE

¼ cup powdered sugar

1 teaspoon nonfat or low-fat milk

⅛ teaspoon vanilla extract

2 tablespoons sliced almonds or chopped walnuts

1. To prepare the filling, place the raspberries and 2½ tablespoons of the juice in a 2-quart pot and place over medium heat. Cover and cook for several minutes, or until the berries soften and release their juices. Combine the cornstarch and remaining juice in a small bowl and stir to dissolve the cornstarch. Stir the cornstarch mixture into the raspberries and cook, still stirring, for another minute, or until the mixture thickens. Stir in the sugar substitute and set aside to cool to room temperature.

2. Place the dough on a lightly floured surface and roll it into a 10-by-12-inch rectangle. Spread the filling over the dough and roll the dough up jelly-roll style, beginning at the long end.

3. Coat a large baking sheet with cooking spray and place the roll on the pan, bringing the ends around to form a circle. Using scissors, cut almost all of the way through the dough at 1-inch intervals. Twist each 1-inch segment to turn the cut-side up. (See the figures on page 174 for clarification.) Cover with a clean kitchen towel and let rise in a warm place for about 45 minutes, or until doubled in size.

4. Lightly brush the top of the ring with the milk. Bake at 350 degrees for about 15 minutes, or until lightly browned and no longer doughy in the center. Cover loosely with aluminum foil during the last part of baking if the ring starts to brown too quickly.

5. To make the glaze, combine all of the glaze ingredients except the almonds in a small bowl and stir until smooth. Drizzle the glaze over the warm loaf and sprinkle with the almonds. Serve warm.

Nutritional Facts (per slice)
Calories: 129   *Carbohydrates:* 24g   *Cholesterol:* 0mg   *Fat:* 2.3g   *Sat Fat:* 0.5g
Fiber: 2.3g   *Protein:* 3.4g   *Sodium:* 78mg   *Calcium:* 17mg
   Diabetic exchanges: 1½ carbohydrate, ½ fat

Orange-Pecan Rolls

1 recipe Whole-Wheat Sweet Dough
   (page 168)

FILLING
½ cup light (reduced-sugar) orange
   marmalade
½ cup chopped pecans

GLAZE
¼ cup powdered sugar
1 teaspoon nonfat or low-fat milk
⅛ teaspoon vanilla extract

1. Place the dough on a lightly floured surface and roll it into a 12-by-16-inch rectangle. Spread the marmalade over the dough and scatter the pecans over the top. Roll the dough up jelly-roll style, beginning at the long end. Cut the roll into 16 slices.

2. Coat a 9-by-13-inch pan or two 9-inch round cake pans with cooking spray and place the rolls in the pan, spacing them evenly apart. Cover with a clean kitchen towel and let rise in a warm place for about 45 minutes or until doubled in size.

3. Bake at 350 degrees for about 12 minutes, or until lightly browned and no longer doughy in the center. Cover loosely with aluminum foil during the last part of baking if the rolls start to brown too quickly.

4. To make the glaze, combine all of the glaze ingredients in a small bowl and stir until smooth. Drizzle the glaze over the warm rolls. Serve warm.

Nutritional Facts (per roll)
Calories: 119 *Carbohydrates:* 18g *Cholesterol:* 0mg *Fat:* 3.6g *Sat Fat:* 0.5g
Fiber: 1.4g *Protein:* 2.6g *Sodium:* 59mg *Calcium:* 12mg
   Diabetic exchanges: 1 carbohydrate, 1 fat

Cinnamon-Raisin Rolls

YIELD: 16 SERVINGS

1 recipe Whole-Wheat Sweet Dough
(page 168)

FILLING
1 tablespoon margarine or butter

½ teaspoon ground cinnamon

Sugar substitute equal to 2 tablespoons
sugar

2 tablespoons maple syrup

¼ cup dark raisins

¼ cup chopped walnuts

GLAZE
¼ cup powdered sugar

1 teaspoon nonfat or low-fat milk

⅛ teaspoon vanilla extract

1. Place the dough on a lightly floured surface and roll it into a 12-by-16-inch rectangle.
2. Combine the margarine and cinnamon and stir to mix. Stir in the sugar substitute, and then slowly stir in the maple syrup. Spread the mixture over the dough and scatter the raisins and walnuts over the top. Roll the dough up jelly-roll style, beginning at the long end. Cut the roll into 16 slices, each slightly less than an inch thick.
3. Coat a 9-by-13-inch pan or two 9-inch round cake pans with cooking spray and place the rolls in the pan, with the cut sides up, spacing them evenly apart. Cover with a clean kitchen towel and let rise in a warm place for about 45 minutes, or until doubled in size.
4. Bake at 350 degrees for about 12 minutes, or until lightly browned and no longer doughy in the center. Cover loosely with aluminum foil during the last part of baking if the ring starts to brown too quickly.
5. To make the glaze, combine all of the glaze ingredients in a small bowl and stir until smooth. Drizzle the glaze over the warm rolls. Serve warm.

Nutritional Facts (per roll)
Calories: 109   *Carbohydrates:* 19g   *Cholesterol:* 0mg   *Fat:* 2.9g   *Sat Fat:* 0.4g
Fiber: 1.1g   *Protein:* 2.8g   *Sodium:* 65mg   *Calcium:* 13mg
Diabetic exchanges: 1 carbohydrate, ½ fat

Index

Also Available from Sandra Woodruff

Secrets of Good-Carb/
Low-Carb Living
ISBN 1-58333-195-6
Paperback

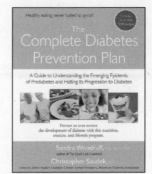
The Complete Diabetes
Prevention Plan
ISBN 1-58333-183-2
Hardcover

The Good Carb Cookbook
ISBN 1-58333-084-4
Paperback

The Best-Kept Secrets of
Healthy Cooking
ISBN 0-89529-880-5
Paperback

Secrets of Fat-Free Baking
ISBN 0-89529-630-6
Paperback

Secrets of Fat-Free Cooking
ISBN 0-89529-668-3
Paperback

Log on to www.penguin.com for more titles by Sandra Woodruff.